Helder's Story:

A Death with Dignity

CAROL GRAHAM PEREIRA

BROTHER MOCKINGBIRD • DIAMONDHEAD, MISSISSIPPI

Library of Congress Control Number: 2018943544

Cover Design by: www.beapurplepenguin.com
For information please contact:
Brother Mockingbird, LLC
www.brothermockingbird.org
ISBN: 978-1-7322155-1-1
First Edition

To Jennifer, Rebecca, Tristan and Rachel.
Dad's legacy of love will live on through you.

Helder's Story:

A Death with Dignity

Prologue

I believe God provides us with subtle messages as we journey down our walk of life. They are found at various intervals on our path. We are graced with these blessings whether we see them or not. Like provisions in a backpack, we pick them up along the way, carrying them around until one is needed. Not until then do we understand why they were placed on our path.

A young boy was walking home one day when a neighbor boy threw a tree pod at him. The pod had small spikes all around it. The boy raised his arm to stop it from hitting him in the face, and by some freak accident, it bounced off his arm, and into his eye with one of the spikes piercing his eyeball. Immediately his eye filled with blood. He was taken to the emergency room; but sadly, nothing could be done for him. Miraculously, after the blood subsided, his eye and his eyesight were fine. Ten years later, the young man started having blurred vision. His parents took him to a specialist, and they checked him into the hospital. Apparently, when they looked inside his eye with their instruments, they could see a plant-like substance, like a root, growing inside. It was remarkable to them. Several ophthalmologists conferred, and they decided to try experimental eye drops, hoping it would kill the plant-like object. They kept him in the hospital overnight, and that evening, a nurse came to see him. She sat with him and said, "You need to visualize your eye healing. Imagine the eye drops slowly killing the plant-like object, and your eyesight getting better." She also told him to think only positive thoughts of recovery. When he left the hospital, he began doing what she said every evening. After three weeks, he returned to the hospital and the doctor examined his eye. All traces of the plant substance was gone.

He never forgot about that experience. He clearly kept that mindset of positive thinking and visualization as well. I know that is how my husband, Helder Pereira, was able to live, for the most part, comfortably and joyously, for twelve years with metastatic cancer.

Chapter One
One Week Prior

Helder came into the kitchen all the way from our bedroom in the back of the house, which was a long walk for him at that point. With metastasized tumors in his brain, bones and both his lungs, it was a difficult task. When he finally reached me, he whispered, "I don't think I can make it until Christmas. I feel like I can't breathe." My husband had lost his voice at that point and was reduced to whispering. The hospice nurses could only guess that one of the brain tumors was resting on a nerve causing problems with his vocal cords. And guesswork is all you can do while on "hospice care." The rule is, no diagnostic tests or scans when you're inevitably not going to do anything about it. This was torture for me.

For twelve years, we lived by the relief of knowing what was going on inside of Helder's body. From there, I worked on a plan to remove or subdue whatever nasty cancer was rearing it's ugly head. I put my arm under his and said, "Well, let's see what we can do about your breathing," and walked him back into the bedroom. I reminded him a low dose of pain medicine would help with the breathing, as well as the bone pain. Helder also had an option to take some oxygen to give him some relief, but I knew he hated sitting with the tubule in his nose. It only reminded him of how diminished he had become. Why force someone who had bravely struggled with stage IV cancer for twelve years to do something that made him uncomfortable? Hospice care is all about making the patient comfortable, both physically and mentally. I told him, "I think you can go one more week. Let's just take it one day at a time and see what we can do to keep you comfortable."

Helder sat in his chair and I sat in mine, next to him. Our tapestry chairs epitomized the classic Ma and Pa picture. He told me that struggling to breathe is unbearable. I knew it was too early in the day for him to start with morphine, so I suggested Ativan. With twenty-eight years of sobriety, morphine was always Helder's last choice. It was cruel and unfair for a man who revered his sobriety to be reduced to taking up to forty mg of opiates daily at the end of his life.

The last month of his brother, Josler's, life left Helder and his parents helpless, watching their sibling (and son) in an opiate stupor, pressing his button for more pain relief whenever he came to. Everyone close to him knew Josler would probably die from an overdose before the lymphoma took him. That was the convincer for Helder. The way he saw it, since many terminally ill patients slip into a drug-induced coma before expiring, why not allow them to die on their own terms? My husband had worked too hard building his integrity and character to have to end his life in what felt like a covert, backstreet way. So, when California Governor Jerry Brown signed the bill allowing physicians to prescribe a lethal dose of barbiturates to end one's life with dignity, my husband asked me to help him get the medication.

California's Death with Dignity law isn't perfect, because the medicine should really be administered by a physician. This would be more humane. Patients have already endured the prognosis of a terminal illness with six months or less to live, with the added burden of putting their affairs in order. Then they are expected to administer the drug *themselves* while they are of sound mind and can still swallow. This restriction is unreasonable. If physicians could administer the drugs on their patient's behalf, there could be more quality time for the patient to live. Swallowing would no longer be an issue. Being physically capable of administering the drug oneself would no longer be an issue. The patient could die without the additional emotional torture.

Helder had no doubt he was making the right decision for himself. At the same time, he was in constant angst over finding the right moment to do it. He said he was afraid he would lose his ability to swallow, as he'd already lost his ability to speak above a whisper. He could feel the tumors in his bones, his lungs, and his brain. He was in constant pain and the end was inevitably near. He had no control over the tumor growth, and no control over how the disease was going to take over his body. But at that final moment, he could decide when and how he was going to die. If prolonging one's life means more time to suffer, it should be at the patient's discretion.

Another timing issue Helder had to consider in selecting a date was finding a time when our four children could be home together. Tristan, aged twenty, joined the United States

Marines, and was in training at the National Geo-Spatial Intelligence Agency in Virginia, with a break during Christmas. Both Jennifer, twenty-seven, and Rebecca, twenty-two, had winter break from their respective schools. Sixteen-year-old Rachel was still in high school and living at home. During this critical time, all four could be home simultaneously. Even so, Helder wasn't sure he could delay taking the medication much longer.

The day after Christmas, 2016 was the day he chose to take the prescription. He did not want to miss that window of opportunity and end up dying like his brother, gasping for air, with his loved ones watching, hoping and praying each breath would be his last. He didn't want that to be his children's last memory of him.

(Back in November, Helder had told our children the time was coming soon, so they could be prepared when that time finally came.) The children asked what we should do that weekend, to make it special, knowing it might be his last Christmas. Helder said he wanted us to to try and have a normal holiday. As was his way, he did not want to be fussed over or treated any differently.

During that last week, it was like walking through a dream. Nothing felt real, knowing that the time was near. We had not yet told anyone, so I kept to myself for a couple of days. I left it to Helder to tell the people he wanted to tell. I was sensitive to the fact that this is a personal decision and that there might be judgments made. Because of his pious religious upbringing, he was very careful who he shared his spiritual beliefs with, so that he neither offended, nor was shamed.

It was as if I were going in slow motion, but time was moving so quickly. How do you "make" quality time when you're on the clock? Then there's the anxiety of saying the wrong thing, accidently hurting feelings. It is difficult weighing your words you say when your loved one has little time left to hear them.

Helder's love for TV really helped him his last days, particularly his love for documentaries and non-fiction. He spent endless hours watching the lives of gorillas, birds, our solar system, etc. It was as if he wanted to take in all he could learn about the world we live in before it was gone for him forever. One night I came into the bedroom and Helder stopped watching TV. He looked at me matter-of-factly, asking if there was anything I wanted to know. I gave him a blank look, though I knew what he meant. After twenty-three years together, were there any dark secrets I needed answers to before I no longer had a chance to ask? I immediately said no. What more is there to know after having discussed his impending death in detail for several years, and what life would be like afterwards? I felt I knew everything I needed to know, which was that we loved each other immensely.

He and I talked about how grateful we were to have had the time to vacation, to spend quality time with our children. We also discussed things that would not have happened if it weren't for his terminal illness. He always said cancer was a mixed blessing. It ended his life too soon; he wouldn't see his children get married, or see his grandchildren, but it gave him an appreciation for life he may never have had.

I had already thought about potential regrets, and I was afraid that there might be something I had forgotten to tell him, and it would be too late. I didn't know what that something would be until that moment. I needed to make a concrete declaration of my love. I said, "The truth is, everything I am, everything you see me doing that you think is so amazing, is that way because of the relationship I have with you. I've always known this, and I want you to know now, that you inspired me to be the greatest person I could be. You allowed me to pursue my desires, whether it was motherhood, a career, or cultivating friendships. It was all inspired by you, because I knew without a single doubt that you believed in me. I have always felt loved by you, and knew that you truly liked the person I was." Choking with tears, I asked him if he knew how much I loved him. He said he did.

The week before Helder planned to end his life, we wondered if any of our children might feel uneasy being in the room when he took the medication. He understood how much love it took to support him in this decision. He still wasn't sure if it was the right thing to ask the kids to be in the room, watching him die. After all, he did not want the experience to have a lifelong negative impact on them. He always grappled with how things would affect his family. Helder had asked each one if they wanted to be there, telling them it was perfectly all right if they didn't. All four said they did. The only other non-family person to be invited was his best friend and spiritual brother, Kenny Lamm.

Helder had asked the kids to refrain from gasping or make crying sounds during those last moments. If they felt like crying, he asked them to quietly leave the room, because he did not want their crying to be the last thing he heard. Nor did he wish to feel guilty with the burden of trying to make them feel better. He wanted to stay focused.

When I was growing up, my family always started our holiday celebration on Christmas Eve; however, Santa Claus coming on Christmas morning was a childhood tradition Helder wanted to pass down to our children. So we compromised, and every year on the 24th, the kids would exchange gifts with each other, and as they got older, they gave us gifts. The 25th was reserved for "Santa's" gifts. After our youngest, Rachel, caught on there was no Santa, we kept the tradition going, so the parents' more expensive and elaborate gifts didn't take the stage over what the kids got for each other, or for us. Christmas Eve was the spiritual part of the holiday, and the 25th was all about consumerism.

The week before Christmas, the kids started asking their father what gifts he wanted. It's almost impossible to describe how strange that feels. What do you get someone when you know they'll soon pass away? How do you ask what they want? How do you even celebrate the holiday? Helder came up with an amazing idea: he asked the kids to write a letter describing their best memories of their relationship with him; that was all he wanted. The kids spent the next couple of days writing their letters.

Throughout that last weekend, they asked me what else they should do. I told them Dad just wanted to be at home. He just wanted to stay low and watch TV. His TV watching had become increasingly intense. If you came into the bedroom to talk to him, he would sigh, pause the TV with a little bit of an annoyance, and then calmly look at you and say, "Yes?" When he did that to me the first time I felt hurt. Are you kidding? It's your last few days and you must watch that show instead of being with me? My women's intuition came through, and I knew he was focusing on something other than the impending situation, so he wouldn't succumb to guilty feelings about his decision. Helder was keenly aware of his codependent tendencies, which included people pleasing. After twenty-six years of recovery in that program, he knew how to set healthy boundaries for himself, so he could keep from putting other people's needs before his own, or "spiral down the rabbit hole" as he called it.

On Christmas Eve, we sat together around the tree, and the kids read their letters to their dad. Each letter was so different; the perspective of each child was unique. Jennifer went first, and told how her dad never gave up on her, as her soccer coach, in school, etc. She said she couldn't have asked for a better father. Next, Rebecca recounted the numerous school field trips, family camping trips, and of course, the zipline he built in our backyard. Tristan wrote about one day having a son, so he could be the same kind of father that Helder was to him. He hoped to pass down the Pereira legacy. Finally, Rachel showed a video on my laptop, before reading her letter. When she was in chorus in elementary school, probably in the third grade, Helder was in the audience videotaping her singing Debbie Boone's "You Light Up My Life" while she signed the lyrics in American Sign Language. In the video, Rachel is singing and signing, casually scanning the audience for her family. Then she spotted her dad and her eyes lit up. You could tell he had done his signature raising up and down of the eyebrows, because she mocked his gesture. She scooted over a little, so she could see him better while she signed and sang. "You," she sang and dramatically pointed to him, "light up my life". We all cried. It was the saddest Christmas Eve I will ever know. Helder was unusually quiet. Of course, he could only whisper. How hard that must have been for someone who loved to talk, who loved Christmas. It had always been his favorite holiday, next to Halloween. At the end of the evening, he told the family he was going to take the medication the day after Christmas. He waited until we were all together; he didn't want to do it until after the holiday. In his whispered voice, he explained his brain tumors were growing, causing him to lose his voice, and he couldn't miss this opportunity while he could still swallow. He said he was in constant pain, and knew the time was right.

The kids joked about how we were going to sleep that last night. One of them said we should have a slumber party in Dad's bedroom with everyone together one last time. The casual banter felt extremely awkward. Helder whispered, "Oh no. Too close for comfort. That's ok." He wanted to be alone. After twenty-three years together, I knew why he was pulling away. He didn't want to get too emotional. I'd learned not to take it personally.

On the morning of the 25th, we got up and gathered in the family room. I had bought some gifts for the kids, and Helder and I watched them open their presents. It was really a formality, so we could emulate our usual traditions. It was an awkward time. I tried to speed it up, so we could get to the family holiday movie, which we voted on every year. This year

Scrooged with Bill Murray won. Helder felt like it was the right movie this time.

I had bought Jamaican Blue Mountain coffee beans for Helder, in memory of our honeymoon in Jamaica. We loved to drink that delicious coffee every morning.

Later that day I made Christmas dinner, and Jennifer's boyfriend, Keith, came over. Tristan's girlfriend, Ariel, and Rebecca's boyfriend, Zachariah, also came. It was a quiet dinner. Since Helder could only whisper, we tried not to ask him too many questions; he said it was exhausting to have a conversation. It was probably the worst dinner I had ever made. I couldn't focus, and everything was either over or undercooked. I had to put the meat in the microwave a couple of times to make sure it was done. Surprisingly, no one got food poisoning. Everyone was gracious about it. Each time I apologized, sweet Zach kept saying, "No, it's good! I like it!" as he poured more steak sauce over the now overcooked steak. Helder stayed until he finished his dinner, and then went to our bedroom to watch TV. The kids had decided to play board games. I went in and sat next to my husband, who was transfixed on a TV program about the galaxy. It felt surreal. We could hear the kids laughing and we looked at each other and smiled. Hands down, one of the best feelings in the world is hearing your children laughing and getting along.

That night Helder told me he was afraid he would start crying in front of the kids before taking the medication, and he didn't want to do that because of how that would make them feel. For the most part, I said very little. I just held his hand; I was numb. I was afraid of what might come out of my mouth. As much as he wanted it this way, including all we went through to get the medication, it was still going to be incredibly difficult to go through with it. Inside my heart, I hoped he wouldn't. I knew this was more dignified than the alternative, but I was afraid of living life without my best friend. This felt like the ultimate show of love for another human being: to hold their hand and love them while they leave you to pass on to another dimension. It is without a doubt one of the most selfless acts our family had ever been a part of. I realized that night my children were very brave, and they had an insurmountable amount of love for their dad to be able to put their own feelings aside to support him.

Eventually each child came in to say good night to their dad. Jennifer's boyfriend, Keith, gave Helder a letter he had written as he said his goodbye. Keith wrote that Jesus was waiting for him, and he would be loved and protected. I got out of bed twice that night to re-read that part of the letter. It was so comforting to hear. I am often touched by the writings of people who feel that close to the Lord. I am amazed and, at the same time, a little jealous.

When it was Tristan's time to say good night, he reminded his dad that he could change his mind. I'm so glad he said that. Although I had wanted to say it, it wasn't my place when Helder wanted me to be supportive. He asked Tristan, thoughtfully, "What then? Would it feel any different one week from now? Two weeks from now? We would eventually be at this same moment." He went on to explain that if he waited, he would run the risk of losing his ability to drink on his own. He was ready.

That night, we went over the funeral service and his final

wishes for the last time. That's when it came to me. The letters our children wrote were so incredibly candid and touching, and truly depicted the essence of Helder. I asked if it was all right if the kids read their letters during the service. None of them had been able to decide what they wanted to say, and I felt the letters said it all. He said it was fine with him as long as it was all right with them. Thankfully, they all agreed. It became the highlight of the memorial service. Before Helder started to crawl into bed, I stopped him to give him a hug. He was deep in thought and preoccupied.

On December 26, 2016, Helder swallowed the mixture in the bathroom, came back into the bedroom and sat in his chair, while I sat next to him. Kenny Lamm was kneeling on his other side. He whispered that angels were preparing a campsite for him. The kids were all sitting on the carpet by his feet. We were all murmuring words of love to him. After about fifteen minutes, He said, "I can start to feel it." We all moved in closer and our words of love came faster and became more emotional. Then he said, "Now you're starting to freak me out." We backed away a little bit. We giggled nervously about his remark and we continued telling him we loved him, holding his hands and feet, letting him know we were there with him. I watched our children, reveling in how close we were as a family. We wanted to be there for Helder, though we were careful to balance it with the amount of emotion he could handle in that moment. Then slowly, but very clearly, he said, "I'm going away now." Those were his last words.

Chapter Two
Helder's Beginnings

His father, Jose, grew up in the countryside of Brazil. One day, members of the Seventh Day Adventist church came to check on his impoverished family. They saw that a young child was hungry, living off what food he could find in the fields. He was being raised by his much older sister. There was never any mention of his parents, so it was presumed that they had abandoned the children.

The Seventh Day Adventists offered to take Jose to live in their parochial boarding school, where he would receive not only room and board, but also a formal education and religious teachings. That was pretty much the end of the story of his childhood as he told it. No other background was given, or known, except the Adventist Church saved Jose from poverty and starvation. It was at this boarding school he met Ester Viana, Helder's mother. She, too, had been taken from her family. She had lived in the country with her mother, who died when Ester was just a few years old. When Jose married Ester Viana, both under five feet and five inches tall, they looked like they belonged on top of their own wedding cake.

They dreamed of moving to the United States of America, where they saw an opportunity to begin a new life, and to start a church of their own. The young couple had two sons, Josler Ignacio, their first born, and three years later, Helder Viana. When she was pregnant with her youngest, the church physician encouraged her to have a homebirth with a midwife. She was told it was more natural than going into a hospital. (Ester always recounted this part of her story with a punctuated, "Ha!")

On March 25, 1962, she went into labor, and almost died. She was in labor nearly all day and night. She would retell, in her thick accent, "We were all tired after the long day, so they used an instrument and tried to open me up like a chicken. Then I heard a loud crack! I blacked out."

Ester was taken to the hospital where Helder was born, and had emergency surgery to have her uterus removed, preventing her from having any more children. Helder was born bearing the brunt of that legacy.

A few months later, Jose and Ester and their two sons, began their journey to the United States where Jose had hoped to become a minister. Fate had other plans for them. Instead of ministering to a congregation, he and Ester served the community by becoming nurses. He usually worked two jobs: one regular, full-time shift in a hospital, and the second, as a private duty nurse in the evenings. Ester worked swing shifts.

Like most immigrants in the 1960s, they felt they were living the American dream, working as much as they could, saving their money, and eventually buying a house in Glendale, California. Jose was known for always ending any conversation with, "God Bless America." Whenever he could, he would send money to his sisters in Brazil. After they passed away, he continued to send money to their daughters. He was vigilant about doing this for them throughout his entire life.

Helder and Josler grew up as latchkey kids. The Pereiras did not know many people when they first lived in California; and they weren't sure how to manage work and childcare. They kept their problems to themselves. They were proud immigrants, working two jobs, and never relied on assistance, whether it was financial or emotional support. Helder remembers being very young, and his brother was probably no more than six years old, when they would be left alone for about thirty minutes between Jose leaving for work, and Ester coming home from work. That was how fearful his parents were about relying on others. When Helder was ten years old, his mother taught him and his brother how to drive a car in case of an emergency. If something were to happen, the boys would be able to drive to a hospital.

Growing up with minimal parental support, the boys learned to rely on themselves at an early age. When they were older, they took on more parental roles. Josler cooked and cleaned; Helder did house repairs and took out the trash. The two brothers became very close, although they didn't always get along.

Jose always tried to be a good father. He took the family on a few camping trips to Yosemite, complete with a canvas tent. Although they worked hard for their money, and scrimped and saved whenever they could, Christmas was a time where expense didn't matter.

The Pereiras lavished their sons with gifts. Helder recalls one year he was so excited he was tearing open gift after gift, barely noticing the present. The sheer enjoyment of ripping off the gift wrapping, one present after another, was their gift.

Another year, Helder asked his parents for a bow and arrow for Christmas. They told him absolutely not. He would surely hurt someone with a dangerous item like that. He was ten or eleven at the time and told his parents he could handle a bow and arrow.

Instead, his parents surprised him and his brother with a TV for their bedroom. In 1972, a TV for your bedroom was an extravagant gift. He was furious with his parents. What they never knew is that he wanted to use the bow and arrow to see if he could shoot it high enough to reach God. That way God couldn't damn him to Hell, like he was told would happen because of his "sinful ways and sinful thinking." Helder had been taught God was literally up in the sky, looking down on him, judging his every move.

As members of the local Seventh Day Adventist church, Helder had to go door to door to solicit literature to neighbors. Two significant principles he learned during this time, which he kept with him his entire life, were to keep his body and his mind healthy. It was by no mistake both of his parents and his brother became nurses. Nursing was not just an occupation, but a spiritual way of life for them. They saw taking care of other people as a gift and a privilege. When the boys were sick, their mother made homemade herbal remedies first, before using traditional medicine. Helder remembered once having a horrible flu, and his mother made a concoction which looked like porridge. She poured it into a cloth, then laid it on his chest. That was one of the stranger home remedies. For the most part, the family was vegetarian and eating healthy was a big part of their life. They believed getting proper nutrition and vitamins should always come from food, not from supplements. Helder's parents did not smoke and had only an occasional drink of alcohol. There is truth to the notion you end up where you started. When Helder had a family of his own, living a healthy life was paramount – physically, mentally and spiritually.

It was a sense of pride for the Pereiras in belonging to the Brazilian Seventh Day Adventist community. Soon though, that pride turned into shame when they could no longer control their younger son. Around age eleven, Helder started sneaking out of the house, and on Saturday nights, taking his parents' car, the one they taught him how to drive, and began roaming the streets. In time, he discovered there was street car racing near the Los Angeles river. This was 1972. The older teens there let him hang around, dubbed him their "mascot" and appointed him to drop the flag to start the races. He loved all of it – sneaking out of the house, participating in illegal car racing, learning how to smoke cigarettes, and the excitement of not getting caught. He embraced the lure of what seemed to be an exciting life, and the acceptance of other teens.

Eventually he got caught, and his car racing adventures abruptly stopped, though sneaking out of the house remained habitual until he was thirteen years old. Prior to this, Helder was having difficulties in school. Not academically; however, he simply could not stay in his seat, follow directions, or adhere to the school rules. He was later diagnosed with Attention Deficit Disorder and prescribed Ritalin. Years later, his parents were asked by the juvenile courts if they were unable to control their son. They gave a simple reply, "Yes." Helder was deemed incorrigible by the authorities, giving the Los Angeles County Juvenile Courts custody of their son. Once again, history repeated itself. Both Jose and Ester were abandoned by their parents; now Helder felt abandoned by his parents.

As an adult, he often said, "My parents tried everything to straighten me out. They even used God against me." He also suggested that this may not have been the teachings of the Church, but rather a tool his parents used to discipline him. He learned that there was something called religious abuse, and he had been a victim. Unfortunately, this instilled a belief in him that God would always hate him for the person he had become, and that all the repentance in the world couldn't change that. It wasn't until much later in his life that he found a loving God, whom he referred to as his Higher Power. Helder saw how much pain he had put his parents through, and no matter how many attempts they made to try and help him, he had always ended up disappointing them. He felt powerless over his behavior; the need to fill the emptiness he always felt inside drove his recklessness.

After Juvenile Court took him away, Helder started a path of self-destruction by getting expelled from schools, including a couple of Seventh Day Adventist boarding schools. He got arrested for curfew violation, running away, and other minor infractions.

One time his parents drove their youngest son down to San Clemente to an Adventist boarding school for boys.

That following Monday, he hitchhiked back to Glendale. This is when he began his drinking and drug career.

The year Helder turned thirteen, two life changing events occurred. First, as a rite of passage, he was reconfirmed and baptized. Second, he completed a sentence in a youth authority camp. The dichotomy in the two events is telling about the two lives Helder was living: obeying God's law, while breaking city laws. He often talked about the ongoing forces of good and evil. This inner turmoil stayed with him until adulthood.

While he was in the juvenile camp, his parents came to visit him with the news they were getting divorced. Helder remembers asking his parents if it was because of him. Despite the fact that they said no, he always felt he was the cause of their divorce.

He always believed his parents did the best they could. One time he found a book they had bought about Aries children. Even though it was against their religion to pursue Astrology, they had read the book, looking for a reason for his behavior, and praying for a solution.

When he was seventeen, the court tried something different, and sentenced Helder to live in the Pacific Lodge Boys' Home in Topanga Canyon. He later said that was the best thing that ever happened to him. The home gave him a sense of worth he never had before. They provided tutors, a psychotherapist, and a structured home life he had never experienced. He went to the local high school and did well, receiving As and Bs on his tests. He was popular, in a good way, and a member of the swim team. One day there was a teacher's strike and Helder organized a student walk out in support of the teachers. Unfortunately, the school retaliated by expelling him. He went back to juvenile court, and they told him since he just turned eighteen in March, he was no longer a ward of the court, and he was sent home three months before his high school graduation.

Helder made one effort to start a new beginning, and that was to enlist in the United States Marine Corps. He felt it would be an honor to serve his country, and by enlisting he could regain the dignity he had lost. When he turned eighteen, he became a naturalized citizen. Helder thought that was all he needed to get his initial application accepted. Unfortunately, possessing a high school diploma was a requirement. At that point, he was too discouraged to pursue a high school diploma or a military career.

Eventually he went right back to his old behavior, except this time he graduated to selling drugs. He sold mostly to the high school crowd, where he became popular for all the wrong reasons. Helder was a natural salesman.

It was the 1980s and there was no shortage of customers. He truly enjoyed talking and interacting with people. He was a people person with a lot of charm. For Helder, selling drugs became an occasion to meet and be with people. With his long curly hair and bright smile, he looked like a cross between Omar Sharif and John Oates of the singing group Hall & Oates. Add in a great sense of humor, and Helder was a big hit.

He had a way about him that made you feel if you only had one friend in the world, he would be the only friend you'd ever need. If you were around at breakfast time, he would make you breakfast; dinner time, pull up a chair, he would serve you.

Helder was the definition of inclusive. He was friends with everyone – tall, short, white, black, thin, heavy, he didn't care. He just wanted to be your friend. That was part of his charm. He had this spark; what the French call, a "joie de vivre," an enthusiasm for life, which made being in his very company exciting. He colored the world around you a little brighter.

Now a single parent, Ester worked nights, so Helder often threw huge parties, charging $5 at the door. This went on for years, and his alcohol and drug addiction got worse. He began getting arrested for being drunk in public. Crashing cars, he eventually resorted to riding his bicycle. His rock bottom got closer and closer. Somewhere during that time, his brother got sober.

Helder spent several years, in and out of jail, taking whatever jobs he could get. Dealing drugs came to a stop when he was arrested for possessing marijuana with the intent to sell. He spent several months in the Los Angeles County Jail. His father brought him a series of books. They didn't mean much at the time, except it gave him something to read.

The books were *The Power of Positive Thinking* and *The Results of Positive Thinking* by Dr. Norman Vincent Peale. Helder often said these books changed his life. He didn't realize it at the time, but the books transformed his way of thinking about himself and his life. Yet, he couldn't completely turn his life around at that time because of his addictions.

While incarcerated, he met a fellow inmate who soon became a friend. This guy also had long curly hair, though his was as blonde as Helder's was black. They felt it was destiny they ended up together, playing out the classic scene of Gene

Wilder and Richard Pryor in the movie *Stir Crazy*. Like the movie, these new friends wanted the other inmates to leave them alone. Helder played 'crazy' well, unzipping his one-piece jumpsuit, and tying the arms around his waist. They survived by staying together and acting like they were out of their minds. The men exchanged telephone numbers, though they never followed through in getting together after they were released until chance brought them back later in sobriety.

The local police came to know Helder on a first name basis. In those days, if you were drunk in public, you were taken to the local police station to sleep it off, and released the following morning on your own recognizance. Gone were the big parties and the dope selling days. He had become a local drunk who scored cocaine when he had the money.

Whenever Josler saw his brother hungover in the mornings, he would ask if he wanted to go to an AA meeting with him. Helder's response was usually, "Why the hell would I want to do that?" His brother always replied, "Just asking."

After Helder got sober he appreciated his brother's firm stance of not involving himself with his drinking problems. He'd often say Josler must have been working a black belt Al-Anon program, or he just knew not to intervene. Helder didn't fully comprehend that his brother was trying to live a sober life while dealing with his drunken escapades, until after he, himself, got sober. Josler never shamed his brother or made him feel worthless because of his drinking. In fact, on those weeks Helder couldn't make enough money for food, his brother would fill up the refrigerator and tell him to help himself to whatever he wanted. In 1983, Josler was diagnosed HIV positive, which eventually turned to AIDS. The full extent of that diagnosis didn't hit Helder until he got sober as well.

Ester remarried and moved out of the house, leaving their sons to live there. Helder converted the garage to a studio apartment, where he continued to drink and use drugs, allowing the bedrooms to be rented out, and he and his brother resumed their roles: Josler cooking and cleaning; Helder making house repairs and doing the yard work.

Helder stayed friends with a girl from his partying days named Lisa. She got sober and was living in a women's recovery home. She had seen the spark in Helder, that joy for life, and was seeing its flame burn low. He recalled that Lisa would call and ask him, "What are you doing with your life?" Then she would invite him to attend AA meetings with her. Helder would tell her he was too busy trying to get his life together to go to any meeting. She persisted and Helder finally agreed he would attend one meeting.

He was somewhat familiar with the AA structure, since he had once been sentenced to five meetings, and three meetings another time, following his arrests for public intoxication. He had always thought attending a "sober meeting" was a punishment you were sentenced to, instead of a place to get help.

Helder never made it to that meeting with Lisa. Instead, he found himself in McArthur Park, one more time, spending his last dollar on cocaine and alcohol. The next day when she called to ask what happened to him, he told her he got busy, doing "stuff" and ended the call.

He remembered sitting on his bed, feeling lost and

alone, and disgusted with himself and his life. He would always remember that feeling of despair. The phone rang a few minutes later, and Lisa said, "Are you sure you're all right?" Helder broke down crying, telling her he wasn't okay. He had experienced that wonderful moment of clarity alcoholics have and told her he thought he might be an alcoholic. On October 18, 1988, Lisa took him to his first voluntary meeting. She was his Eskimo. An Eskimo is the person who leads you into your first meetings to begin the twelve-step program.

After going to a few more meetings together, Lisa told him he needed to find a "drudging buddy," someone who could take him to meetings. She suggested a mutual friend of theirs who had recently gotten sober. The problem with this connection was that he and Helder had been in a physical fight years ago at school. At that time, the friend was a scrawny kid; however he had grown into a much larger man who could surely retaliate. Helder had no choice, so he rode his bicycle to the guy's house and knocked on the door.

The man stepped outside onto the porch. Helder in his fear mixed with grief, broke down crying, and yelled, "I'm an alcoholic! I need your help!" The man replied, "Calm down man, and get in the house. I have neighbors!" He lovingly put his arm around Helder and brought him inside, with eyes darting around for nosy neighbors.

Chapter Three
Sobriety

A friend Helder had met in the "program" later recalled that when she first started going to AA meetings, she dreaded attending. But, at the time, she noted Helder standing on the sidewalk in front of the meeting hall. She recalled, "Here's this guy, telling jokes, drawing a crowd around him. They are all laughing and having a good time. I thought, 'That's who I want to hang around with!' And it was just Helder's third day!"

Helder was most comfortable being the entertainer, the life of the party. He had a way about him that captivated audiences. He was blessed with the ability to bring that with him into sobriety. With his new family of sober, broken souls, riddled with despair and hopelessness, there was no shortness of people for him to entertain. Helder went to at least one meeting a day, sometimes three. He soon fell in love with the 10 p.m. candlelight meetings. The lights were turned off, and the only thing visible were faces aglow from the lit candles, prompting people to share their most vulnerable feelings in a non-threatening atmosphere. He loved the emotion he felt in those rooms, connecting with others on a deeper level.

So much of his persona as the "entertainer" was on a superficial level. Helder craved a deeper relationship with people.

Later in life he recognized what he felt was God's love in these late-night meetings. Afterwards, he usually went to the local coffee shop with other members, staying late, swapping "war" stories, and sharing the eventual path to sobriety. The "meeting after the meeting" it was sometimes called. At one point he was told the program wasn't just about fellowship. He needed to work the steps. He needed a sponsor.

One guy, Bob, always asked Helder if he had found a sponsor, if he had started working the steps. Helder would reply with a grin, "No, not yet. I'm working on it." Then Bob would respond, "You're going to die if you don't get one, mother-effer!" This went on almost every day.

At the celebration of his thirty-day chip, Bob asked him again, "Did you get a sponsor yet?" Helder, feeling like he was raining on his parade yelled, "No not yet! Why don't YOU be my sponsor?!"

Bob asked him, "Are you willing to go to any lengths for your sobriety?" The coffee shop got quiet. Helder was still suspicious of the program and new-found way of life. Ever the conspiracy theorist, he thought, *here it comes. Everything comes at a price.* He had had to do a lot of things he didn't want to do to get his drugs and alcohol. He figured the same must happen with sponsorship. With his fingers crossed behind his back, he yelled, "Yes! I am willing to go to any lengths for my sobriety!" At that the group cheered and went back to their celebration. Helder almost always told that story in his AA "pitch" in later years. He had never before experienced a true friendship where nothing was asked from him. This was true about the love and encouragement he received not only from Bob, but from everyone he met in the program. It was a new way of living, which touched him deeply.

Right from the beginning, Helder wanted a life companion badly. He was constantly on the search for "the one." Once he thought he had found a special woman until he saw her kissing another guy before a meeting. He skipped the meeting and went directly home, heartbroken. Suddenly a knock came at the door. It was his cocaine dealer. "Helder, open up! I have some new grade of coke!" Helder's first thought was, "Great, this is what happens when you skip a meeting!" He yelled back, "Leave me alone, man. I don't do that anymore." After several tries the dealer eventually stopped knocking. He looked for his new sponsor's telephone number, written on a napkin from the coffee shop, and realized he had been using it to wipe his tears. He was desperately trying to read the blurry number when suddenly, he heard knocking again. "Go away, man. I told you I don't do that anymore." At that point, he started to feel everything was going wrong and the answer to his problems was literally knocking at his door. Then he heard, "It's me, Bob. Let me in." Helder swung open the door and his heart lifted when he saw his sponsor standing there.

Bob said, "You're just starting out in sobriety. Once you start working on yourself, there won't be just one, you'll have lots of girls to pick from." This sounded like a pretty good proposition to Helder. Then he said, "I know how you can get this companion you're looking for. I have a sure-fire way that will make this happen for you. First, I want you to write a list of everything you want in your ideal woman. Go into detail and write down all the qualities she should have." Helder did this, and after several days, leaving out no details, came up with five pages of things he wanted his perfect companion to possess. Bob looked at it and said, "Now, once you have these qualities in yourself, she will appear." Helder started crossing out qualities and tore out whole pages. His list got a lot shorter.

Eventually, someone told Helder about another program, Co-Dependents Anonymous (CoDA). This program is for people who yearn to have healthy, loving relationships. It was apparent to him that he didn't know how to do that. In the program, Helder discovered the most important relationship was the one he had with himself. That relationship was almost non-existent. All his life, other people had defined who he was. He looked to others for gauging his feelings and self-worth. He worked so hard at not being alone, connecting with people, that he never developed a relationship with himself.

Helder jumped into this program, and it was the first time in his life he did something for himself, by himself. None of his peers from the other program joined him. When he went to that first CoDA meeting, he knew he had found the solution to his loneliness.

For the first time in his life, Helder learned to do things on his own, like going to the movies or out to lunch. He even went camping by himself. This process gave him a whole new dimension. Not only was he charming and able to make other people feel good around him, but he developed a sense of confidence and self-esteem he never had before. The awareness he learned became very attractive, and once again, people were drawn to Helder, this time for all the right reasons.

He soon had a core group of friends he went everywhere with. They went to dances, dressed up for Halloween parties, played volleyball at the beach, and even went skydiving. The skydiving adventure was a result of his friendship with a fellow AA member, a skydiving instructor. He offered the first lesson for free to entice new skydivers. That's all it took for Helder. He jumped five times out of a Cessna airplane with a static line, which pulls the parachute line for you, then he was qualified for a free fall.

Out of all his new adventures, Helder's favorite sober activity became Campvention, a camp-out and convention in one! Campvention was for sober people, complete with meetings and workshops, and a Saturday night dance, at a massive campground in Lake Perris, California. Hundreds of people gathered for this annual three-day weekend, camping near the lake. This is when Helder first started accumulating camping gear and pursued his love for the outdoors. Having grown up with Angeles National Forest just a twenty-minute drive away, camping had been a part of his life before sobriety, and now he was able to make it a big part of his sober life. He always yearned for the outdoors, feeling a connection with nature.

Slowly, Josler and Helder integrated their individual lives and created a family home life. One tradition they started was their annual Pre-Thanksgiving Potluck Party. They invited everyone they knew to celebrate a holiday meal with friends. It was always held the Saturday before Thanksgiving, which was often a difficult holiday to spend with family. No one was excluded, and friends of friends were welcomed. This tradition carried on every year for twenty-eight consecutive years.

Another tradition the brothers started together was

Christmas Eve midnight service. Josler had become involved with the Episcopalian church in Hollywood. They accepted his sexual identity, so he felt comfortable worshipping there. He always invited his brother to attend with him. This started Helder's journey back to church, and to discovering a God of his own understanding. It was a journey to replace the punitive God his parents portrayed with a more loving, merciful God.

The two brothers did their best at keeping those traditions that felt like family and home. Helder invited everyone he knew to Christmas Eve services at St. Thomas Church. He loved inviting friends who would not normally attend regular services, let alone midnight services. He enjoyed broadening his friends' spiritual views, and wanted to show them they had a right to worship, no matter where they were on their spiritual journeys. He loved bringing broken souls, who thought they weren't welcomed, into the security of the sanctuary.

Helder's financial situation began improving as well. He first started working for a carpet cleaning company, but after winning Salesman of the Year his first year, he branched out and started his own company, Allcare Miracle Carpet Cleaning. *Little did he know starting his own company would be the conduit for meeting his future wife.*

The business became quite successful, and added house cleaning as a service offering. The main ingredient was Helder. He treated his customers as friends. He had a way of connecting with people no matter the circumstances. In turn, his customers would tell him their stories: why they needed their carpets cleaned, how they purchased their house, where they bought their furniture, even what their kids were like, the history of their wine stains, their blood stains, their dog and cat stains. Helder would discuss philosophy, books he'd read, and current events. Some of his customers even became close friends. Helder saw it as more than just a business, it was a service he provided to help people. One Sunday, a frantic caller explained he had seen Helder's advertisement and needed someone to come over as soon as possible, for house cleaning and carpet cleaning. When Helder got to the house, the man who answered the door looked horrible. He was unshaven, red-eyed, and reeked of alcohol. His wife had left him and was seeking a divorce and custody of their daughter.

The man had achieved fourteen years of sobriety until this had happened. He was reeling from a weekend binge, and explained he needed help with the house immediately, because his wife was bringing their daughter to visit the next morning.

Helder walked through the house with his assistant, Ronoldo, a friend of a friend who recently arrived from Brazil. There was vomit and diarrhea everywhere on the carpet. The kitchen sink was filled with unwashed dishes, which were also covered in vomit. When they got outside, Ronoldo told Helder the conditions were disgusting and vile, and he couldn't be in the house. Helder said, "Hey man, we can't leave this guy like this. Nobody else will clean this up. He needs our help. We have to go back in there and clean it up!" Somehow Helder was able to convince his employee, and they cleaned the house. When they were done, Helder gave the customer his personal home number and told him he would take him to a meeting if he called.

Another time, Helder received a call from a band manager. One of the band members had gone on a binge over the weekend, and they needed him to clean their Hollywood penthouse apartment. When he got there, the musician was crawling around the carpet, looking for something. He had written lyrics and music on pieces of napkins, matchbooks and on the back of envelopes. The problem was, the entire floor was covered in trash, empty beer bottles and cans. He had thrown a party, and his work got strewn all over the apartment. Some of it had been thrown in the trash.

Helder spent several hours painstakingly going through the mounds of trash on the carpet, and the trash cans, picking out anything that looked like lyrics written on scraps of paper. Needless to say, the musician was very grateful.

Through his business, Helder met people from all walks of life: airline pilots, actors, sheriffs, and with each one came a story. As time went on, most customers became repeat customers, and he was able to stop advertising.

Helder's business increased, and it was time to hire more staff. At an AA meeting, a new member, Marty, said he needed work. Helder told him he could hire him if he was willing to learn carpet cleaning. Marty said the only problem was he didn't have a car. So, Helder picked him up for work. They ended up spending a lot of time getting to know each other and reminiscing about their pasts. One day over lunch, Marty said, "You know, I didn't always go by my current last name. I used to go by Marty so-and-so." Helder said, "I knew a Marty so-and-so! I met him in jail when I was in my twenties. We became friends and acted like we were crazy, so we wouldn't get jumped!"

The men looked at each other, realizing they had met many years earlier under different circumstances, and shouted, "What are the chances?!" Marty said, "I thought you looked familiar" and they both laughed. Ironically, both men had cut off their long curly hair, and wore crew cuts! Marty became one of Helder's closest friends. Sponsorship is the cornerstone in the twelve-step programs, and Helder sponsored Marty for nearly twenty years.

Helder told that story often, driving home the point there are no coincidences in life. He was a firm believer that people came into your life who were meant to be there. That spurred him into being a man of action. He would always say, "Look for the miracles."

He was very pragmatic when it came to starting new relationships with people. Helder didn't care where you came from or where you'd been. It was that attitude and open-mindedness that led two former inmates to reunite, some twenty years later, which goes in line with one of Helder's favorite concepts, the Six Degrees of Separation.

The idea is that, because we are all linked by chains of acquaintances, all living things are six or fewer steps away from each other, so that a chain of "a friend of a friend" statements can be made to connect any two people in a maximum of six steps.

Another person Helder believed was divinely put on his path was Scott H. It turns out, Scott was also raised with a Seventh Day Adventist upbringing. Sponsoring Scott, and eventually becoming great friends with Scott was another male bonding relationship for Helder. Eventually they started an annual men's camping trip which included Marty and others.

Helder's business began taking off again, providing a better income. He bought a dirt bike, a jet ski, and a pickup truck, all within a couple of years. He soon discovered sobriety came with benefits, like the ability to maintain a steady job.

Everything that was purchased was with the intention of sharing with friends and family. He took his jet ski to Campvention and used it at Lake Perris. Days were spent on the lakeshore, riding his jet ski, and offering it for others to ride. Other times, Helder would put it in the back of his pick-up truck and drive to Ventura Beach by himself. There he could launch the jet ski into the ocean and jump the waves. When he lived at Pacific Boys Lodge, he taught himself how to surf, so being in the ocean was easy for him. He also taught himself to snow ski, among other things. Anything he needed to learn he taught himself. Like his parents, he rarely asked for help.

Helder loved the outdoors and everything there was to do there. He would bring his dirt bike camping, usually to Hungry Valley, where he would let his friends ride it. One particular friend, Jim G. would ride with him. Some of his fondest dirt bike riding memories were when he was newly sober and riding with Jim G.

In 1993, when Helder had four years of sobriety, his dear friend, Kenny Lamm, sold a condominium to a single mom. The carpets were filthy. He promised the woman he would give her contact information to a fantastic carpet cleaner. That woman was me. Right after I purchased the condo, Kenny gave me Helder's number. I trusted Kenny's opinion. After all, he was the husband of my friend, Julie Lamm, a friend from work. She had told me Kenny was a realtor, and would help me find the perfect condominium that would fit my small budget.

(What I didn't know was that Julie, who was Brazilian, also knew Helder. Many years later, we discovered that Julie's mother went to the same Seventh Day Adventist college in Brazil as Helder's parents. *Six Degrees of Separation*.)

I called Helder and we arranged to meet before I had to be at my office at 8 a.m. He was late. Jennifer, my three-year-old, and I were waiting outside the condo for him, while I was rehearsing the reprimand I would give him about his being on time, and my being late to work. I'm pretty sure I was tapping my foot, when suddenly I saw this guy walking toward me, which looked more like skipping, down the pathway. He had long brown curly hair, big brown eyes, and a thousand-watt smile. I don't think I'd ever seen anyone smile so brightly in my life. His energy reached me before he did. At once I forgot that he was late and that I would be late. It suddenly felt so insignificant in comparison to the wave of cheerfulness brought to the morning. He had a pleasant, upbeat energy about him. It was instantly infectious.

Helder introduced himself and shook my hand. Just a few minutes prior I was so angry about his being six minutes late; the quick change in my own attitude took me by surprise. I could barely shake his hand. "Shall we go in and look at the carpet?" he asked with that never-ending smile. A genuine smile. Not a salesman's "I want to make a sale" smile. It was a "Here's a new person I get to meet!" smile. We walked through the condo, addressed the carpet problems, and after some discussion, agreed on a price.

We were both sitting on the steps inside my new condo, and Jennifer was swinging on the second-floor railing. As a single mother, I had to bring my daughter with me while looking at condos, signing loan documents, enrolling in a new pre-school, and getting the utilities turned on. It had been a hectic few weeks, squeezing all that in and working a full-time job. I didn't realize it at the time, but later when I thought about it, there was a feeling of calm and tranquility in that moment when the three of us were just sitting there, with the early morning sun shining through the window. It felt like home. Suddenly, as Helder was writing up the invoice, and I was relaxing in the moment, Jennifer blurted out matter-of-factly, "Is he going to be the Daddy?"

Chapter Four
Our Family

Immediately, there was a "Before Helder" time and an "After Helder" time in my life. It felt like I had been living in black and white until Helder entered my life; suddenly, I began living in vivid color. At first, we began a genuine friendship. He asked me about some books he had seen on my bookcase, *The Road Less Traveled* by M. Scott Peck and John Bradshaw's, *Healing the Shame that Binds You*. These were books you wouldn't find in most people's libraries.

We discovered we had a lot in common. One night he made a list: we were both vegetarian, loved camping, we both got sober at twenty-six years old, we were both in therapy and completely infatuated with each other! We spent hours talking about the books we'd read, sometimes into the wee hours of the night. We soon discovered we were both interested in the book, *A Course in Miracles*. Our first "outing" was Marianne Williams' lecture on *A Course in Miracles* at the Wilshire Ebell Theatre. We didn't consider ourselves dating because of my daughter's role in our relationship. Her birth father moved back to his home in Georgia when she was five months old. She was too young to remember him. With this in mind, and no father figure in her life, Jennifer was a big factor in our dating process that we didn't take lightly. Thus, our relationship was purely platonic at first, but there was unmistakable chemistry. That was just fine with me. Helder was such a fun-loving person, and I could see he was a loyal friend. I was happy just securing my way into his inner circle of friends. Then, out of the blue, Helder's father invited him to go to Brazil, and off he went for an entire month. While he was there, he took the message of *A Course in Miracles* with him. The course teaches love and miracles are in everything, as well as everywhere.

Helder experienced his home country very differently than when he had been there three years earlier, and this trip was just the second time he had been back since leaving. Not once did Jose and Ester take their sons back to Brazil after they left the country. The reason for this visit was because Jose had remarried, and they were visiting his new wife's relatives.

He had always made a point to visit his sisters out in the country and bring them whatever he could fit in his suitcase. This time it was a typewriter! Helder couldn't believe it. His father actually packed a manual typewriter, because Jose had gotten his first electric typewriter, and he didn't throw anything away. He either stored it or sent it to his siblings back home.

Helder saw everything in Brazil as a miracle; from the village where his Dad's new wife grew up, to where the people got their water supply which was from a nearby spring. There was no running water, and people slept in hammocks nailed to the interior walls of their small houses.

It seemed everyone in the village had children, and although they were not all married, they all seemed happy and content. Later Helder would share how that made a big impression on him. He played with the children, and they followed him around the village as if he were the Pied Piper. It was an incredibly spiritual experience for Helder to see this community of families, sharing their lives with their children. It was so different from the childhood he knew, with both parents working day and night.

Helder was also reading *The Road Less Traveled*, which addresses the importance of healthy parenting and raising children. During his stay in Brazil, he made the decision he wanted to pursue a relationship with me. I remember the day he called me from airport customs, a collect call from a payphone. He said he missed me and thought of me often. He also discussed an awareness he discovered while he was away.

Our romantic relationship started. We went camping, dirt-bike riding in Hungry Valley, to sober picnics, and for the first time for me and Jennifer, to Campvention in Lake Perris. In November of 1993, Josler invited his brother to a potluck lunch at his church, St. Thomas Episcopal in Hollywood. Helder invited me. We attended a worship service before the lunch.

I remember standing next to Helder while we were singing a hymn, when suddenly he reached over and laced his fingers in mine. It was a turning point in our relationship; a very bonding and spiritual experience for us, holding hands, singing in church with the one you love. Helder began reconnecting with good feelings about religion.

Jennifer turned four that year, and Helder began picking her up after preschool for playdates, so I could run errands. I had never wanted to date before, because for me as a single mom, it would only be to find a husband for me and a father

41

for my daughter. I had no interest in a boyfriend, nor did I want someone in Jennifer's life that might be temporary. Child raising was an important matter to me, so I didn't see any reason to date someone.

Helder took parenting seriously. He believed a person's childhood was a sacred time, and he started addressing his relationship with Jennifer in his own therapy sessions. He wanted to be a healthy role model. I had never met anyone who took the impact they have on a child so seriously. He wanted to make sure he said the right things, so he was always positive and nurturing. Helder and I stayed away from labeling our relationship. Calling each other boyfriend or girlfriend felt like it didn't really give it the weight it deserved, and most definitely didn't address the Jennifer factor. It would have sounded too superficial in comparison to what we three had together.

In the meantime, Helder talked me into the skydiving package. I jumped five times with a static line, which took several months, then on January 16, 1994, I did my last and final jump, a free fall.

On January 17th at 4:55 a.m. there was an earthquake measuring 6.7 on the Richter scale. It was centered in Northridge, about ten miles from where I lived. Jennifer and I held each other in bed, waiting for aftershocks. All of a sudden, I heard a knock on my door. With flashlight in hand, and a toddler on my hip, I opened the door. There was Helder in his heavy all-weather jacket, standing six feet tall and carrying a monster-sized flashlight, asking, "Is everyone all right in here?" We jumped into his arms. That was the moment I knew he would be my protector.

That following week there was another historic event. I missed my period. I invited Helder to come over to my place to discuss the situation. He lived at 1234 Grandview, and I lived at 456 Magnolia. My good friend Suzi Salvi, who had been studying numerology at the time, pointed out we were connected. Later that common number four became our family's lucky number.

Helder suggested I take some time to really think about what I wanted to do with the pregnancy. He already knew, but he wanted me to be certain of what I wanted since it wasn't planned.

I visited Marianne Williamson at her home in West Hollywood and told her the situation. We prayed, talked, then talked and prayed until I knew what to do. When Helder and I met again, I told him I wanted to have this baby. It would have been nice if the circumstances were more traditional, but they didn't turn out that way. Helder held my hand and very formally told me he was committed to me, to our baby and to Jennifer, one day at a time, for the rest of his life. Being a hippie at heart, and in a spiritual phase of my life, it was all I needed to hear to feel I was having my baby in a committed, loving relationship. In my heart that verbal commitment from Helder held more weight than any traditional ritual.

He moved into my condo the following month, and soon after, said he wanted to get married. *Let's get married!* I was willing to take our state of affairs on the road and run to Vegas for a speedy wedding. I quickly learned Helder had very specific wishes when it came to marriage. First, he wanted a traditional ceremony in a church, preferably St. Thomas, the Apostle. Secondly, he didn't want to rush the planning. He felt a good wedding would take time to plan, and he didn't want me walking down the aisle showing six or seven months pregnant. There was a surprisingly conservative quality to Helder. We didn't get married until after our daughter, Rebecca, was born, because he wanted things done in a certain order. He wanted to propose in the traditional fashion; and to plan the wedding of our dreams. Most importantly, he didn't want any of it to feel rushed or hurried or done out of shame. He wanted everything to be done out of love. I'm so glad he did, because it unfolded exactly the way he envisioned it.

Helder was extremely involved with my pregnancy. He bought me a portable water filter, so I could filter water wherever I was, including restaurants. One time I caught a flu, and he was adamant that I not take aspirin or over-the-counter medicines. He said natural remedies were best. I was miserable going to bed that night, so he insisted I drink sixty ounces of water to flush the flu out of my system. All night long he poured me glasses of water. The next day my fever broke, and I started to feel better! When my allergies started acting up, Helder bought a homeopathic allergy remedy, which went under my tongue, and they worked as well as prescription allergy pills.

Helder would not allow me to lift anything or strain myself in any way. When I was about six months pregnant during the summer, we went to a pool party and he was worried about me being out in the sun. He was afraid I would have a hard-boiled baby. Helder made my lunch every day for work, which started a twenty-year tradition. He became the lunch maker in the family.

One day we were walking through the mall in Burbank; I was pregnant with Rebecca and Jennifer was holding my hand. We saw an American Youth Soccer Organization (AYSO) table with a sign-up sheet recruiting soccer players. I thought it would be something Helder and Jennifer could do together, so I registered her and saw there was also a sign-up sheet for volunteers. I put his name down as a volunteer. A few weeks later, he received a phone call at home, asking if he would like to coach his daughter's team. I was thrilled, but he wasn't. Helder told the caller that while he loved watching the sport on TV, this Brazilian had never actually played soccer. The caller said "No problem. We have coaching clinics. All you need is the willingness to learn." That is how Helder started his twenty-two-year career in coaching AYSO soccer. He eventually coached all of his children, and one year, he coached three teams during the same season.

Helder also became an AYSO referee, often volunteering to referee games on days he didn't have a game. At first, he didn't like to referee games. Most people don't. Of course, he learned to be diplomatic, and he grew to love everything about soccer. Nothing thrilled him more than watching his children play. He was barely able to contain his enthusiasm for the game. Helder loved to encourage everyone, not just his own children, but other children as well. You could always count on him noticing how well a player controlled the ball and shouting "Good job!" If a goal was scored, Helder would give a play by play recount of the goal.

Then, Josler started to get very sick. Reflecting back, Helder felt once he moved into my condominium to start a family of his own, Josler's body surrendered to AIDs, which had already taken a toll on him physically. Helder felt his brother stopped fighting the disease once he knew Helder had the security of his own family.

Josler had offered to throw us a baby shower, and he kept that promise. He threw a huge co-ed baby shower at their childhood home, complete with fun and games. At the party, he had already started losing his equilibrium and was walking with a cane. It was apparent his health had taken a turn for the worse. That was in August 1994. Eventually, it was discovered Josler had also acquired brain lymphoma.

This terminal diagnosis caused him to be hospitalized in the hospice unit of North Hollywood Presbyterian Hospital. Josler's last weeks were torturous for Helder. Every day he visited the hospital only to find him in horrible pain. His brother had been a nurse, like their parents. He knew that the pain and suffering would be unbearable. Not just physically for him, but for his parents to watch the slow progression of the disease. That is why Josler included in his Advance Directive to withhold food and water to hasten his death. This isn't an unusual wish for terminally ill patients when there are long periods of suffering. He cared less about his own pain than he did about his parents' suffering. Their pain was compounded by their own guilt, as they assumed it was all their fault. He knew they didn't understand the disease or his sexuality. What he did not anticipate was how tortured his parents would be watching him starve to death.

At first, his parents thought it was a mistake. They kept arguing with the nurses, telling them it was inhumane not to feed him. He tried to explain that he requested the directive some time ago, knowing that his health would deteriorate to the point where it would be merciless to try and keep him alive. But to his parents this was wrong on many levels. They worked so hard all their lives to provide for their son, and now he must starve to death? It was unconscionable. They stayed by his bedside crying day and night.

Helder was filled with mixed emotions. Our daughter, Rebecca, was born on October 4th. How could he be elated for his beautiful, new baby girl, while his brother was suffering in the hospital? He, too, cried in the hospital day and night. The nurses told Helder not to worry, because without nutrition, his brother would eventually administer a lethal dose of pain medication via the self-medicating pump. It would soon be over. But it wasn't. It went on seemingly forever. Helder said each day felt like a week, each week felt like a month. He hated himself for wishing the end would come soon, so that his parents could stop being tortured, and he could stop feeling guilty for his happy life with his new baby girl. When Josler finally died, on November 16th, Helder had stepped out to go to an AA meeting. After all those countless hours by his brother's side, he wasn't there when he passed. Although it was AIDS related, the reality was that his brother, sober for fifteen years, died from a combination of starvation and an overdose of morphine. Helder felt it was an undignified way to die, and it planted a seed for him.

Josler was cremated and interred in the wall of the chapel at St. Thomas Episcopal Church. Helder and I attended the memorial service, while our two children stayed at home with our babysitter. Helder lost more than a brother. Josler had been his primary caregiver, confidant, roommate and surrogate domestic partner at various times in his life.

Thirteen days later, Helder proposed to me. He took me out to dinner for my ten-year sober anniversary. Between the entrée and dessert, he put a napkin on the floor and got down on one knee. Later he said that Rebecca and Jennifer had gone with him to pick out the engagement ring.

We got married at the church where Josler was interred. With him gone, and the roommates having moved out of the house, their childhood home was empty. Jose was living with his second wife in Glendale. Ester, now a widow, had inherited her second husband's house and lived in Los Feliz.

She surprised us one day by gifting us the two-bedroom, one bath house, to make a home for our family. We moved in and immediately started making renovations. Nothing had been updated in the home since they purchased it in the 1960s. We put in central air conditioning, a paved driveway, and new carpet and paint. Then, Helder promptly designed a treehouse.

Jose had planted a tree when they first bought the house, and it grew into a magnificent maple tree. Helder's two-story treehouse even had ropes, so you could swing from the second story out into the yard, and then jump off.

We were married on June 10, 1995, and had a vegetarian meal reception at the church reception hall. All our friends were invited. One of Helder's friends, not in the sober programs, said that he had never been to a wedding where no alcohol was served, but everyone was on the dance floor until late into the evening.

Helder planned an amazing honeymoon in Jamaica,

and we had a fabulous time. He took scuba diving lessons and fell in love with it. When we returned from our honeymoon I discovered I was pregnant. Rebecca was eight months old, and we were overjoyed. I explained to Jennifer now that I was married, I was changing my name to Pereira. She wanted to be a Pereira too. When I told Helder, he asked what needed to be done to adopt her. We started adoption proceedings, and with little fanfare, Helder adopted Jennifer, and her name was changed to Pereira.

Then we received some bad news. While we were on our honeymoon, Jose had been very depressed about the loss of his son months before, and took a handful of sleeping pills and drank a large amount of wine. He was taken to the hospital to have his stomach pumped. The doctors were concerned and put him on a seventy-two-hour watch hold. Fortunately, he had stayed involved with the Seventh Day Adventist Church which seemed to help ease his pain.

Helder was a natural father. As soon as we discovered this pregnancy he forbade me from exerting myself in any way. He would tell me to just sit and relax. "I'll take care of it," was his constant response. He was first in charge of changing Rebecca's diaper, picking her up when she cried in the middle of the night, and getting her back to sleep. We lived close to Brand Park, so we often walked there with Rebecca in the stroller. Helder had a way of soothing a crying baby. When there was no consoling Rebecca, he would take her in his arm and simply walk outside to the maple tree. Usually holding her outward, so she could look at everything. Almost instantly she would stop crying, mesmerized by what she saw. Nature was Helder's go-to remedy for every ailment.

We both had read a book by Robert Johnson, in which he referenced the story of Tristan and Isolde. In the story, Tristan was known for his loyalty and bravery. We chose that name for our son Tristan, who was born on Valentine's Day in 1996.

Once we were three, and we quickly grew to five, adapting to the change along the way. Being a small business owner, Helder had the flexibility to be Mr. Mom, while I worked full-time in legal management. His day started at 5:30 a.m. to get a jump on things, and continued that way for most of our life together. He made breakfast, then lunches, and dropped the children off to daycare and school. From there, he went to his first job, where he finished up around 2:00 p.m. His second job began when he picked the children up from school, went grocery shopping, made dinner, and did laundry.

Having had plenty of practice growing up, Helder was a natural at these things. In between, he also had soccer practice with Jennifer, attended his meetings and never forgot our date night on Saturday nights. Family life was a dream come true. Holidays were done up big, especially Halloween. It should be a national holiday as far as Helder was concerned. For many years he loved dressing up for Halloween, adding costumes to his collection each year. Now that he had children to dress up, he was ecstatic.

We started going camping as a family, first at Campvention, then by ourselves. Helder packed up the portable crib, sleeping bags, camping equipment and one big family tent for all of us to sleep in. When I was pregnant with Rebecca and then later with Tristan, Helder did all the packing up and setting up camp. He was a one man show.

In 1998, Helder got the idea to buy a boat, so we could take it camping and go out on the lake. I objected, but he searched the classified ads, and eventually found a 1991 Bayliner, only three years old. He was determined to bargain with the owner, so he could bring the price down to our budget. For Helder, negotiating was an art form; a sport which he loved playing, good-naturedly. For years he would tell us, "Don't say anything while I'm bargaining." Yet every time, we would pipe up, "That's a good price, Dad! Take it!" We were known to foil his strategy.

Helder went to look at the boat, with cash in hand. As luck would have it, the seller recently got a job working in the entertainment industry building sets. A single man with no kids, he was bringing home money hand over fist for the first time in his life. He had bought the boat on a whim, but soon realized he didn't have the time or interest in keeping it. Helder made him an offer he couldn't refuse. My husband was blessed with the gift of gab when it came to closing a deal, and came home with a boat, a boat trailer, new water skis, and a couple of life vests for half the price it was advertised.

We spent almost every summer weekend going up to Lake Piru, a forty-minute drive, keeping the boat docked at Castaic Lake. We bought inflatables to pull behind the boat. In the boat's cassette player was a reggae tape, and somehow, we could never remember to bring any other tapes. Summer weekends were filled with Bob Marley's music out on the lake with the kids. It became an inside joke for us, and after a while we associated boating on the lake with reggae music. We invited friends whenever possible. Helder took the boat on his annual men's camping trip to Lake Mohave with Scott, Marty, and a few other close friends.

One time we invited Jennifer's soccer friend and her family, the Yamamotos, on the boat. Years later they mentioned that weekend was one of their favorite family memories, going out on the lake. Helder loved that. He saw boating and camping as a conduit for building family and friend relationships. Sharing his good life with others was the best part of living to him.

Chapter Five

Kemper Avenue

In 1999, I found out I was pregnant again, with Rachel. Helder and I were thrilled. One more time, he took on most of the responsibilities. He wanted me to concentrate on taking care of myself and the baby. At the time, Jennifer was ten, Rebecca was five and Tristan was four. All three were registered to play soccer. In addition, Rebecca was taking dance lessons, Jennifer was ice skating, and Tristan had joined the Cub Scouts. In the Spring there was Little League baseball and girls' softball. It was always a busy and fun life.

Helder's business continued to do well, and it seemed he took on more than he could handle at times. Every night, he thanked God for his sobriety and for the family he always dreamed of having. One day, Helder mentioned to me he had blood in his stool. After four pregnancies, all I could think of was hemorrhoids, and told him it was probably that. He wasn't one to worry about his health, but after it happened a few more times, we agreed he should see a doctor. A proctologist did a physical exam and confirmed the bleeding was not caused by hemorrhoids. We put our worry aside and went on living our life.

On December 31, 1999, we threw a sober New Years' Eve party and invited everyone we knew to bring in the new millennium. The house was full of people, laughing, talking and spilling out into the backyard. They were friends from meetings, the neighborhood, along with a few childhood friends. Yes, we were all sober when we did the countdown at midnight. We told the kids they could stay up until midnight, but the two youngest, Tristan and Rebecca did not make it.

Rachel was born on February 18, 2000. She looked and acted just like an angel. She barely cried and slept most of the time. When Helder brought the kids to the hospital, each one sat in the big mommy chair and held her. It was a tender moment. They were all old enough to understand there was a new baby in the house.

The day we brought Rachel home, it was just the three of us, and we sat on the couch with our new angel, peaceful in her baby carrier. We were sitting there, admiring her when Helder said, almost sadly, "We could have had one more." He knew that wasn't going to happen because I had gotten my tubes tied right after the delivery. I was forty-one years old. He was sad knowing that she was going to be our last. After his comment, and looking at the baby's angelic face, we dubbed her Rachel, the Angel. After all, only a baby so heavenly could inspire someone with four children to say they could have one more.

We were outgrowing our two-bedroom house and had already added a bedroom/office. With a fourth child, it was going to be a tight squeeze. We had a dilemma whenever we considered selling the house. How could we even consider selling the house that Helder and his brother grew up in and made a home for themselves and their friends? It was also the house the Pereira grandchildren were growing up in, while attending the same schools as their father and uncle. It was very difficult for Helder to make that decision taking all that in to consideration. On top of that, the garage and attic were packed with all the items family had left behind.

When my father passed away in 1996, Helder inherited his belongings. Dad grew up in the Depression and saved every item he ever owned in his garage. When he died, my mother said she would just as soon light a match to the garage. To her it was full of junk. The saying "One man's junk is another man's treasure" was written with Helder in mind. He hurried over to the house and quickly packed nearly everything into his work van and brought it to our house in Glendale. It broke his heart to think my father saved and cherished these items all his life to have them given or thrown away without being appreciated. My father saved a die cutting tool set from the 1950s, antiques from the 1930s, along with gadgets, doodads and contraptions. These were all gems to Helder.

My father and Helder's father were a lot alike in that they grew up in poverty, and nothing was ever thrown away. In addition to that, we kept all the household items the elder Pereiras left behind when they divorced, and all Josler's belongings when he passed away. Moving would be a huge undertaking. Once again, our realtor friend Kenny came to the rescue. At first it seemed impossible to find a house that Helder would like: it had to have room for our boat, a good-sized yard, at least four bedrooms, and it had to come within our middle-class budget. I suspected Helder was making it difficult to find the right house because he was having a difficult time leaving the home he grew up in.

One Friday, Kenny found an upcoming sale of a house in La Crescenta, just ten minutes north of Glendale. He told us to "Run, don't walk!" to look at this property. He said it would go on the market days later and predicted contractors would want to make offers right away to buy it and build two houses on the flat 22,000 sq. ft. lot.

On Saturday morning we went to look at the house. Trees were overgrown in the front yard, which had a broken chain link fence. The swimming pool was empty except for a small greenish puddle at the bottom. It also had a large crack on the plaster. The backyard was full of dead fruit trees, and most of the windows were broken. Inside the house, which had been abandoned for almost a year, were huge cobwebs throughout. The master bedroom, a poorly made illegal add-on, had a broken wood-burning fireplace because the house had no heating system; and the unfinished basement had water seeping through the cement walls. We both saw something different. We saw the seven sixty-foot historic deodar cedar trees on the lot. We saw the stone rock foundation around the house. Most of all, we saw our children growing up in this house. We saw birthday parties in the backyard; our annual Thanksgiving party with people filling up the basement. We saw room for our boat, jet ski and dirt bike trailer. This house was nothing like any of the previous houses we had seen. And so, our vision came to pass.

The house was within our budget, but we would have to sell our Glendale house and my condominium to afford it. We gambled everything we had to get this house. I had the same vision as Helder, except I wasn't sure how we would get there. My only concern was how were we going to be able to fix the house up after spending everything we had on buying it. It needed a lot of repairs and had one less bedroom than we needed! Still, Helder told me that wasn't going to be a problem. He said if I could figure out the financial part to get us into the house, he would be able to fix it on our tight budget. And I knew that Helder could do anything once he put his mind to it. By Sunday night, we signed the purchase agreement and were the proud owners of a two-bedroom, one bathroom, broken-down house on a half-acre of land. When we showed the house to Ester, she cried, and said in her best English still saturated with Portuguese accent, "Please don't buy this house, it looks like it's going to fall down and kill you!" The kids pulled on our arms crying, "Why can't we get one of those other houses we looked at, without the spider webs! We can't live here!" They couldn't see what we saw.

In September 2000, we moved into the Kemper Avenue house, and had our first Thanksgiving Open House two months later, amidst drop cloths and plastic tarps. It did feel a little like living in the haunted house on the street, which was zoned as a private street, with *No Trespassing* signs. Neighbors came over to see who had moved into the broken, abandoned house.

Almost immediately, Helder applied for a construction permit as owner-builder and started interviewing sub-contractors to do the work. About that time, two young men, Edmilson and Flavio, friends of friends from Ester's church, arrived from Brazil and were looking for work. They were both studying theology and needed to earn some money. They helped us move from Glendale to La Crescenta, packing boxes, moving furniture, and sometimes just holding the baby. Helder oversaw every aspect of the house remodel. He even rented a bobtail truck and landscaped the backyard, removing the dead and dying fruit trees.

Eventually he had blueprints drawn up, and hired an independent sub-contractor to act as foreman and build the foundation and framework. Helder knew a lot about building, but he had no experience reading blueprints. Soon, the sub-contractor stopped showing up at the house. Eventually his workmen came knocking on the door, asking Helder to pay them their wages. When he asked where their boss had been, they said he was in jail for public drunkenness. Helder told them he should have been released by now. Apparently, the foreman was in the country illegally and would probably get deported.

One workman spoke up saying he was here legally and could probably finish the job if given the opportunity. He said he could read blueprints a little, and between him and Helder, they figured out how to build the rest of the house. With the help of a very kind and friendly inspector, they added four bedrooms and four bathrooms to the house. It was a shaky beginning. When the rebar was first laid down, the county inspector came to approve it before cement was poured. He scratched his head, and soon realized the rebar had been put in upside down. That about sums up how the construction went, trial and error. Each phase of the home expansion had to be reviewed and approved by the inspector. Thankfully, he was so impressed with Helder's willingness and passion to learn, he would let him fix any errors and come back to approve them once they were fixed.

And there were quite a few errors! Fortunately, people wanted to help Helder, because he was willing to put in the effort to help himself.

There were other problems. The basement appeared to be leaking water from outside the house, where there was soil. Helder got the idea to dig up all the dirt surrounding the outside of the house and pour concrete there instead. Then he did some research and found a product that was known to stop water from coming through the cement block. He applied that to the inside of the house in the basement. After a short while, it was apparent his idea worked. Helder had many more creative construction ideas, and the 4,500 sq. ft. house was built just under budget.

Two other Brazilians tiled the bathrooms, and other day laborers he hired worked on drywall. Helder loved giving people the opportunity to earn money. And he always worked right alongside of them. That was his trademark. He hired an apprentice from the electrician's union to do all the electrical work. The job was completed, although some of the switches in the house were turned on in the opposite direction.

Before putting sod in the backyard, Helder discovered a lot of rocks and boulders had been buried under the dirt. He found a cheap way to get rid of them. He decided to build a rock wall in the backyard. Helder visualized it, and Flavio and Edmilson built it. It was most definitely a Zen-like project. The rocks had to be put in a certain arrangement in order to stand about three feet high and approximately thirty feet long. The first time it had to be redone. Off and on the three men would stand back from the wall, and just stare, trying to get the right "feel" of it. Helder was very proud of the finished product. Most people who came to the house asked if we hired a landscape artist to do the rock wall. Helder always replied, "Yes, all the way from Brazil!"

The people he hired to work for him were often brought into his life and treated like family. Flavio and Edmilson had never been water skiing, so of course, Helder invited them on the boat and insisted they try to water ski. We all had a fun time watching. It bonded them with our family forever. The men were invited to Rebecca's reptile-themed sixth birthday party in October of 2000. We had hired a host who brought reptiles, including an albino boa constrictor. Flavio and Edmilson told us we were without a doubt the most "interesting" family they had ever met.

By the summer of 2001, the house was complete; however, it was always a work in progress. Soon after, Helder decided to take the family on a trip to Cabo San Lucas. He insisted on inviting his mother, his father, and his father's second wife, Elia. Helder wanted his children to spend as much time with their grandparents as they could, even if it meant bringing his divorced parents together. Family vacations were never complete without his parents, and they agreed with the arrangement. It gave Helder great pleasure to see his parents enjoying his children; playing with them, feeding them, and holding them. His parents never interfered when it came to parenting the kids, which made vacationing with them that much easier.

By the end of 2004, life was in full swing. The kids were fifteen, ten, eight, and four. Helder always ran his carpet cleaning business throughout the years, though he never allowed it to get in the way of family life. He had very specific parenting values, as well. He loved his parents very much, but it was clear in his mind that he wanted to raise his children differently. Since I worked full-time in downtown Los Angeles and came home in the early evening, Helder made sure he was there to pick the kids up from school. Unlike his own childhood where he was home alone most of the time, summer vacations for his children were spent supervised either at Camp Pereira with Dad as the camp counselor, or a few weeks here and there at summer YMCA camp.

Every year, each child had a birthday party at the house. I added it up and by the time they were eighteen, that was fifty-two birthday parties held at the Kemper house! Helder had a standing rule: each student in the classroom had to be invited throughout elementary school. There were times the kids protested, and with good cause. They weren't always friends with everyone in the class or sometimes their classmates just didn't like them. Their dad always responded, "If they're not your friend, then they won't come to the party. But you must at least extend the invitation to them. You cannot leave certain kids out. I know how that feels and no child should feel left out."

As the children got older, Helder started a tradition that each birthday party should include games: bobbing for apples, potato sack races, and always, musical chairs. When Rebecca had her thirteenth birthday party in the backyard, she said, "Dad, I really don't want to play games this time. We're too old for that. And I really don't want my parents or my siblings to be hanging out with my friends." Her objections fell on deaf ears. It was an unusually warm October day, so Helder decided to include the "water balloon toss" game. He split the kids up so half were facing each other, and after each toss, they had to step two feet away from each other. It was videotaped and ended up being one of our favorite home videos to watch. Everyone played, including the siblings, and we all had a lot of fun. Rebecca's friends thought it was a great idea! Helder had an uncanny way of bringing out the child in everyone, including thirteen-year olds filled with angst.

At this point, Helder was coaching three soccer teams, volunteering in the school classrooms, and filling in as a field trip driver when needed. Tristan had been in Cub Scouts since first grade, and his dad often volunteered the backyard to have overnight "camping" trips for their Cub Den. Every soccer season ended with a team party, and Helder insisted on having them at the house. At the end of the school year, he started organizing a "Last day of school pool party" which started off just around our pool, but grew to include a rented water slide, the kind you see at park carnivals.

Jennifer's soccer team practices were usually the last time slot in the evening, usually on Friday nights, so the older teens didn't stay out late on a school night. Helder got the idea one time to go to Shakey's Pizza Parlor after Friday night practice. Anyone without a ride came with him in our eight-seater SUV for pizza and camaraderie. They all liked it so much it was repeated a couple more times. Helder told me he liked to provide a safe place for the teens to go on a Friday night. He often worried that the kids, whether it was his own or others, would take that wrong turn, and head down the road he did as a teen. He knew being bored on a weekend night could possibly lead to trouble. Since the other teen coaches didn't like to take Friday night slots, Helder usually volunteered for them.

Movies were an essential part of our family life. Helder had spent hours watching TV growing up as a child, and watching movies on the big screen was one of his favorite outings. There was usually a movie to mark a special occasion; whatever movie was coming out around your birthday, that would be your "birthday" movie. While most were Disney and Pixar, there was also room for Harry Potter and other fantasy films. Helder was just as excited as the kids when a new movie came out, and it always thrilled him to watch the upcoming trailers. He loved the places movies could take you to, and the fantasy you could live in just for those couple of hours.

Halloween was like a national holiday in the Pereira household. We all dressed up, and trick or treating was the evening's big event. Rain or shine. We spent many Halloween nights with umbrellas over the kids' heads. Helder collected Halloween decorations year-round.

That first year we moved to La Crescenta, we received a flyer from the children's elementary school regarding an annual Halloween parade for the kids. All children should dress in their costumes for the parade. Helder dressed up as well; he was the only parent who did. Six years later, when Rachel started going to school there, many parents dressed up, even the teachers! Helder had a way of breaking the ice and giving people permission to bring out the child in themselves.

That year, he went as Captain Hook, because Tristan, who was four at the time, had picked out a Peter Pan costume. We went to Hollywood's Halloween Parade, where the street is shut down, so people can parade down the street. At one point, a crowd gathered around them, and they performed an impromptu fight with Helder saying loudly, "I'll get you yet Peter Pan!" The crowd adored it and cheered on Peter Pan, giving them both a round of applause. Helder loved that night, and he absolutely loved participating in the children's childhood.

One day not long after that, Helder said, "I don't want to scare you, but there's a lot more blood now. A lot." He went back to his primary physician who scheduled an appointment for him to have a sigmoidoscopy.

Chapter Six
It Begins

On January 5, 2005, Helder went to his gastroenterologist for a procedure called a sigmoidoscopy. It is similar to a colonoscopy except that it can be done in the doctor's office without any anesthesia, allowing the patient to be awake while viewing the procedure on the screen. It's not as thorough as the colonoscopy; however, if you're suspecting hemorrhoids, it does the job. I received a phone call at work from Helder later that morning:

> "I just got out of my appointment."
> "How did it go, Helder?"
> "He told me I have cancer."
> "What?! If this is a joke, it's a really bad one."
> "That's what he said. 'You have cancer.'"
> "How could he tell so soon?! Don't you have to do a biopsy or something?"
> "Apparently it's so obvious he could tell right away."
> "Maybe you misunderstood."

We never saw it coming. We never had a moment to prepare ourselves. And the doctor's appalling bedside manner made it even more shocking. While Helder was on the table having the procedure, the doctor told him he saw a tumor. Helder asked, "What does that mean?" The doctor replied, "It means you have cancer."

After Helder got off the table, he asked the doctor what he should do. The doctor replied, "You should walk out this door, go across the street to the hospital, and have a barium x-ray to confirm. In the meantime, I took a sample of the tumor for a biopsy and will have the results in a few days."

After Helder and I hung up, I instantly remembered that during medical insurance open enrollment in December, I had just switched from PPO to HMO type insurance effective January 1st. I thought we could save a couple hundred dollars a month in premiums, and after all, no one in our family *ever* gets sick! Remembering this decision made me go numb with fear. What I didn't know is that we ended up saving hundreds of thousands of dollars in the long run. Case in point, one of my work partners whose wife had cancer ended up having to sell his house and withdraw his oldest child from an Ivy League school in order to pay for his wife's cancer treatments. In the end, for us it turned out to be a miracle and one of the best decisions I ever made. Everything was covered at 100%, as long as we were knowledgeable about our choices and didn't mind the never-ending telephone calls to the insurance company to get authorizations and second opinions.

That night Helder and I held each other close. Our heads were spinning from the possibility that he actually had cancer. The days before we received the final results felt like life stood still. We were holding our breath waiting to hear there was a mistake. I called the doctor's office the next day for the results, and they explained they needed Helder's permission to discuss his case with me. That was how it went from there on out. I would fax over Helder's authorization to the physician to discuss his medical treatment with me, then I would pass the results onto Helder. He never once called a doctor's office for results. Not once. He would rather hear the news from me than from a stranger.

Helder had no patience for dealing with doctor's offices, being put on hold, and possibly not getting the answers in a timely manner. All that felt demeaning to him. Being healthy was an important element in his childhood, especially having a mother, father and brother in healthcare. Their belief was that good health was the result of good living; eating healthy, and taking care of your body, mind and spirit. Therefore, being physically compromised felt wrong. It is said that life has a way of smoothing out your rough edges. If the shame of being ill was a rough edge, God sure found a way to smooth those out for Helder. The upside of having me as his advocate was that it allowed him to stay focused on living his life to the fullest. From the very beginning, I told him just what he needed to know. I believe this philosophy allowed him to keep his positive attitude. It removed the intricacies of managing his own healthcare, creating a necessary buffer from the reality of living with cancer. We were both keenly aware that this was one of many blessings he was to receive on this journey.

After a few days, we got the results. The tumor was positive for adenocarcinoma. He had a three cm tumor, located one and a half cm from the anal verge. Helder was diagnosed with colorectal cancer at forty-three years old. I immediately asked for a copy of the biopsy report be faxed to me. That became regular protocol for us, to always get things in writing.

That night we told the children. We were sitting around the dining table which Helder had made, and he announced he had some bad news. He said they found a tumor in his colon and it tested positive for cancer, yet he was hopeful and didn't know how bad it was yet. Rachel, just shy of her fifth birthday, covered her face with her little hands, and put her head down on the table, saying, "This is very, very bad news." The kids got up and gathered around their dad hugging him, telling him they loved him.

Telling the children had been difficult; but telling Helder's parents was unbearable. It had been ten years since their oldest son had died from AIDS. Now their only living child was diagnosed with cancer. It was almost too much for them to bear. Helder could see the guilt and shame they carried from his brother's death come back all over again. They carried that skewed religious belief that somehow, they were the cause, and God was punishing them.

Helder saw a surgeon who recommended he get a 3D scan because of the location of the tumor. The purpose of this diagnostic test was to get an image to see how deeply the tumor had invaded the colon and if any nearby lymph nodes had been penetrated. At that point his diagnosis was stage I cancer. I remember waiting in the hallway for the radiologist, so I could get his initial feedback. He told me it looked good and that the tumor hadn't invaded surrounding lymph nodes or grown outside of the colon. Eventually we received confirmation of that initial consult. All good news! We were so hopeful! Already at that point, we felt the shift in how we related to each other, and the grace that settled into our daily interactions with our family. After being faced with cancer, we became softer with each other. We became a little kinder, a little more forgiving. Suddenly we had a vast amount of patience for each other and in our daily life. The best part was that Helder still had his sense of humor. One night around one o'clock in the morning, Rachel had a bad dream and called out for Mommy and Daddy. I turned over in bed and said, "I'm so tired." Helder replied, without missing a beat, "I have cancer." We both laughed. I remember feeling like we hadn't laughed in a while and it felt good. One more time, Helder put some levity into a very challenging situation.

I called ahead to the surgeon's office to make sure they had the x-ray which was needed for our next appointment. They didn't. That meant we had to drive first to Burbank, a thirty-minute drive, to pick up the x-ray then hand carry it to the surgeon's appointment in Glendale. That interaction set the stage and put into motion how we handled my husband's journey with cancer. As the patient, Helder was overwhelmed with just having cancer. We knew then we had to be proactive, and that his health depended on it. There was no room for balls to be dropped or information to get lost in the shuffle. Hand-carrying those x-rays emphasized we had to be vigilant in following through with scans, x-rays, reports or whatever was needed to decide on the next step of his treatment. We could have the best team of surgeons, oncologists, and physicians, yet we had to take the lead in *coordinating* Helder's care ourselves. Later, when he joined a cancer support group, Helder was appalled at how many cancer patients relied on their healthcare team to coordinate their treatment, and they themselves were not proactive about their own care. He took it upon himself to enlighten anyone afflicted with cancer about his own discoveries and experience.

Once at the surgeon's office, he told us he could remove the tumor entirely with a minimally invasive procedure called a transanal excision. He said Helder would be able to go home that same day.

One night when Helder was putting Rachel to bed, I overheard him tell her not to worry. He told her by the time she was five years old, his cancer would be gone. Her birthday was on February 18th. The surgery took place on January 25th. Helder ended up staying in the hospital overnight because of excess bleeding due to the depth of the cut to remove the tumor. We were both taken aback, but I realized at that point; even though you may have a scan or an x-ray, it's only when the doctor is in surgery and can see with his own eyes, that you truly know what's going on inside the body. This became a recurring theme.

We went to the post-operative appointment with the surgeon and were given the bad news. There were no clear margins. We learned when removing a tumor, it's important to have a margin of cancer free tissue removed along the rim of the tumor. Otherwise, cancer cells can be left behind following tumor removal. That's all it takes for the cancer to continue growing.

Dr. Silcott recommended a resection of the colon. This would entail making an incision through the lower abdomen, removing a section of the colon, just before and after where the tumor had been. We sat in his office stunned. Helder had been convinced he had a *little* cancer, and it would be removed. That would be the end of that story. A resection of the colon was a major operation and required a hospital stay for several days. Helder tried to justify not doing the surgery because there was a minimal chance the cancer ended right where the incision margin was, with no cancer left behind. As a safety measure, chemotherapy was already planned as a post-surgery standard protocol to kill any additional cancer cells left behind. We sat in Dr. Silcott's office for a long time until finally it felt like a coin toss decision. The doctor said, if it were his ass, (he had the same sense of humor as Helder), he would go back in and do the resection. Another benefit of performing the surgery was that during the operation, the surgeon could collect some lymph nodes to make sure they were free of cancer. Helder was anxious to get it over with, so we scheduled the resection for March 28th, three days after his birthday. One more time Helder had to complete a bowel prep, his third in two months. A bowel prep requires fasting for twenty-four hours and drinking a laxative, called "GoLYTELY" to ensure the bowels are completely empty.

At USC Verdugo Hills Hospital, Helder was distraught but hopeful all the cancer would be removed this time, and the resection would show a clear margin. After the surgery, Dr. Silcott came to the waiting room and told me it was a success and there was a nice-sized clear margin. "I really think we got it all," he said.

Those are the magic words you want to hear! I brought the kids to see their dad later that evening. He was in a lot of pain and extremely uncomfortable. He asked me to take the children home. I clearly remember him saying, "Just take care of the children." Even in his opioid haze, Helder felt ashamed of not being the person he knew his children remembered. Later he told me it was a nightmare being on the pain medication. Being in that state of mind was worse than anything he had experienced since being sober, which was seventeen years at that time. Helder disliked the feeling that he was no longer in control. He lost the ability to clearly communicate what was in his mind, as if he were trapped inside his brain. It felt like a living hell. Helder realized that he had taken for granted how good it felt to be completely aware mentally and in full control of his body physically. What he didn't know is that he would have to experience that hell again and again over the years. What he couldn't possibly imagine is that morphine would one day become a daily necessity.

Two days after the surgery, I was in Office Depot picking up school supplies when Helder called my cell phone. Dr. Silcott had been in to see him with the biopsy result. It showed four of the nine lymph nodes had been invaded by cancer. The cancer had metastasized. We hadn't anticipated more bad news. I knew from my research that the lymph nodes are the body's highway system; whatever is in a lymph node can travel throughout the body. I also knew that this meant Helder immediately went from stage 1 to stage III. If one or more lymph nodes are invaded by cancer cells, you are at stage III. I dropped the school supplies and quickly went to the hospital to be with Helder. I ran to his bed and held his hand, telling him how sorry I was. That's when he cried. For the first time since his diagnosis he cried. He had been so hopeful that this was the last bowel prep, the last doctor's visit. He had thought he would be done with cancer. I had Tristan with me, and he stood next to his dad and held his other hand.

Dr. Silcott was still there, and I asked him what the next step was. He said this changed their plan of attack. Helder would have to complete twenty-eight days of radiation and see an oncologist to start chemotherapy as soon as possible. He also recommended an ileostomy. This is similar to a colostomy except it's placed higher up. It entails having the surgeon open the abdominal cavity, cut the intestines, pull them out from an incision on the side of the body, where a stoma is created, and a pouch is attached on the outside of the stomach to collect stool. The stool is averted from where the surgery took place in the rectum, and Helder wouldn't have to endure the pain from the diarrhea, a common side effect of both radiation and chemotherapy. This would be most excruciating at the surgical site. The doctor asked if Helder had any questions. He asked, "Will this interfere with coaching soccer?"

The ileostomy was scheduled for April 5th. During the procedure, they would put a portable catheter into a main vein in the chest wall. This would allow intravenous fluids which would normally go through the vein in your arm, to go through the portacath.

Helder endured twenty-eight days of radiation scheduled Mondays, Wednesdays and Fridays with weekends off. At the first visit with the radiation doctor, Helder sat close to me, wrapping his arm around mine, his head on my shoulder. The doctor asked, "Are you in pain, or are you holding onto your wife for emotional support?" Helder replied, "Both. I am in constant pain, so I'm holding onto my wife for emotional support." If I could have melded my body into his at that moment I would have, to give him the strength he needed to endure the post-operative pain. My husband had undergone three surgeries in almost as many months. This doctor gave Helder his first lecture on the importance of addressing his pain. He told him that pain management would allow his body to heal quicker and explained how addressing the pain early is a very important factor in the quality of his life. Helder said he understood, though he did not want to take pain medicine unless he "really needed them."

Eventually I went back to work, and Kenny often took Helder to his radiation appointments, as did several neighbors. He always got the love and support he needed from friends and neighbors. Helder started chemotherapy right after the radiation was completed. One of the weekly infusions took several hours at the oncologist's office, so they gave him the "chemo suite" with a VCR to watch movies, and a bathroom conveniently located across the hall, so he could go throw up, on cue, immediately after the infusion was completed. That took place weekly from April until November.

The other chemo drug had to be infused slowly for several hours at a time, around the clock. Helder had to carry a "5x7 inch" black box around with him which contained the chemo. It had a strap he wore around his neck like a cross-body purse. The infusion tube went from the box into his portacath. Every now and then you could hear it start up with a low whirring sound. At this point, Helder had lost thirty pounds.

Spring soccer began, and Helder couldn't coach. There was a lot of sadness surrounding his cancer progression, but what made it most difficult for him was not being able to coach. He still went to all Jennifer's, Rebecca's and Tristan's games in 2005. His AYSO (American Youth Soccer Organization) family learned of his cancer and chemo treatments, and openly showed their love and support.

Although Helder couldn't coach, he still tried to keep up the momentum of his soccer family life. When it was time to have an end of season team party, he insisted we have it at our house. It was after spring session, so it was warm, and he decided to make it a swim party. I thought that was too much to put on us, but all the parents helped; even though Helder did a lot of work setting up for the party, greeting families, and making sure all guests were enjoying themselves. As was his way, Helder not only invited team players, but all the siblings too. Almost everyone showed up for the party and all had a great time. After a few hours, I was running from the kitchen to the pool area when I noticed Helder wasn't around. I found him in our bedroom, lying down on the bed. "What are you doing?" I exclaimed. "We are having a party and you're lying down!" All I could think of was all the people he had invited over, and how much more of an entertainer he was than I was. He replied, calmly and slowly, "I'm a little tired. I think I need to rest." Just then I heard the whir of the chemo box. I had forgotten he was having chemo treatment during all of this! There was a pause, then I said, "All right. You can take a short nap. Come out when you're feeling better. I love you." Our eyes met, and it was understood. Helder appreciated me not treating him like a sick person; that I expected him to participate in our lives. I like to believe it kept him going during those times when he thought he couldn't.

That summer we didn't take the boat out and there were no camping trips. Helder spent a lot of time playing video games and watching TV. He was grateful for his constant companions. During this time, our neighbors and friends came through miraculously. Arrangements were made so that we had homemade dinners prepared and delivered to our family of six Monday through Friday for several weeks.

I remember one night, the Taylors, who lived two doors down from us, brought us steaks, baked potatoes with all the trimmings, and salad. Then a few hours later, I heard a knock at the front door. It was pouring rain and we wondered who it could be. When I opened the door, two of the Taylors' young daughters were standing there with a tray of warm brownies. We were very loved and never once felt alone during this time.

Fall soccer season started up in August of 2005, and Helder coached Jennifer's team in the U16 (under sixteen) division. Rebecca and Tristan wanted their dad to coach their teams and were outwardly disappointed.

After Helder completed chemotherapy, and the diarrhea stopped, he wanted to reverse the ileostomy. That surgery was performed on December 5th. It was not successful due to the extreme pain it caused Helder. At the annual talent show at Monte Vista Elementary School, which was scheduled just after his procedure, Helder had to sit in the back row, running to the bathroom several times. He had lost control of the muscle allowing him to hold his stool. It was physically and emotionally uncomfortable for him. Helder told me that excreting on himself was the most degrading and horrifying experience for him.

After several weeks, he asked for a temporary colostomy, so that he could have more time to heal.

The oncologist began monitoring Helder's blood carcinoembryonic antigen (CEA) level. When the CEA level rises in patients who have had colon cancer, it is an indicator that the cancer may have metastasized or there has been a reoccurrence. In the spring of 2006, just a few months after his temporary colostomy, Helder's CEA level started rising; a CT scan was ordered, and a tumor was found in his liver. At that point, I asked for the results as soon as they were available, not waiting for a doctor visit. It felt like his life was on a timer and waiting for doctors was a luxury we no longer had. I asked Helder how much he wanted to know about his prognosis. I had read that some people prefer not to know. He wanted to know only on a "need to know" basis. He asked if he should prepare for the end. I told him that evening that he had stage IV cancer. "How many stages are there?" he asked. I told him four stages. He looked at me, stunned, "Are you sure? There aren't five?" He was serious. I explained the criteria for stage IV is having more than two lymph nodes affected by cancer, venous invasion by the cancer, and the cancer metastasized to a major organ. In Helder's joking fashion he said, "I'm in big trouble now."

Sadly, the diagnosis came just when he had started living an almost normal life. He was working, coaching soccer, and planning to coach two teams that season so he could coach Tristan and Rebecca. He thought it was time to spread his coaching skills around. Having your father as your coach is a mixed blessing. Helder demanded more from his kids than any of the other players. He expected them to be first to practices, warm up before the practice, help set up the field, and help clean up. He also kept them in the game longer and expected them to keep playing until they were taken off the field on a stretcher.

One of our family funny lines was, "You're not going to start crying, are you?" Once Rebecca was injured and fell onto the ground. Helder was already short players, and down several points, so he didn't want to lose Rebecca to an injury. When a player is down, the referee stops the game and assesses the injury to determine if the player needs to come off the field. The referee signaled for Helder to come out to discuss the situation. In her dad's "enthusiasm" to keep Rebecca in the game, and fear that the referee was going to send her out, he shouted on his way across the field, "You're not going to start crying, are you?"

All the parents within earshot looked more than a little surprised. Helder was embarrassed later by his outburst, but not for long. He explained, "I know Rebecca is going to give me her best because she's playing for me, and that makes her invaluable." The pride went both ways. The kids loved having their dad coach them because they knew he was passionate about soccer: coaching, playing or refereeing. It was more than a game to him. It was a way of life and a sport which brought the family together every Saturday and Sunday.

On May 5, 2006, Helder had a liver resection, after Dr. Silcott and Dr. Carvajal, the liver specialist, met with us to explain the importance of removing the entire rectum, and the surrounding colon. They explained that since the cancer had metastasized to the liver, there was a high probability it might have already spread to the original site, even though it was not visible on a scan yet. The only way to lower that risk was to remove his rectum. He still had plenty of colon to live a healthy life; still, it would mean having a permanent colostomy. Helder struggled with the decision for several days. He wasn't sure he was ready to commit to a permanent colostomy. When I started to force the issue of having the surgery, he retorted, "I don't want to feel pressured into doing this or any other procedure if I'm not comfortable! I need you to support my decision without making me feel guilty. I'm the one who has to live with the results." After that, I never pressured him again. I would give him all the facts and let him know I would support whatever decision he made. My husband was right, I didn't have to live with the outcome. In the end, the deciding factor was the survival rate. Helder had a 60% chance of survival if he had the surgery. "Survival" is code for living cancer-free for at least five years. We started living five years at a time. Once he made his decision, he never complained about living with a colostomy. Not once.

Helder was extremely anxious going into this surgery. He went over his wishes if he didn't survive the surgery. One of them was to buy Jennifer a Volkswagen he had researched on Autotrader. Even with all his worry about removing his rectum and living with a permanent colostomy, his last words before going into surgery were, "It's a good deal. Please get the car for her."

When the doctor later came to the waiting room, I was given the good news that they successfully removed the tumor from his liver and, "It looks like we got it all." Later, the biopsy taken from the rectal area showed a new nodule. Clearly it was the right decision to have this surgery.

In early spring of 2007, less than one year after his last surgery, Helder's CEA level started rising again. Another scan was performed, and a new tumor was found in his liver. Months prior, it had been suggested to get a second opinion from the City of Hope (a comprehensive cancer center), but we felt that was too "dramatic". Earlier on in his battle with cancer, we were both afraid to pursue anything that felt like the disease might be here to stay for a while. This time we decided to visit City of Hope. When we walked into the lobby, it felt very strange for Helder to be there. Seeing so many patients wearing scarves on their heads or masks on their faces made the battle with cancer a reality. What we didn't expect was for Helder to qualify for a new clinical drug trial. The doctor overseeing his case was a liver surgeon who specializes in metastatic colon cancer. Bingo! The trial was for a new radioactive chemotherapy. First they removed the tumor, then Helder started the trial chemo. He had a second surgery in which they removed his gallbladder. This allowed them to insert a device where the gallbladder used to be, which infused chemotherapy directly into the liver (hepatic intra-arterial chemotherapy).

During the chemo trial, Helder received radioactive medicine. Because we had young children at home, the decision was made to let him stay in the City of Hope village for a couple of months. Radioactive medicine made him a risk to other people as well as himself since his immune system was compromised.

The team who brought food and cleaned his room wore Hazmat type clothing, so they would not be exposed to the radiation. Helder had to stop working, and he had no disability insurance. His mother, distraught beyond belief, withdrew money from her life savings to give her son an amount equal to his annual income, so he could take off work for a year. He could concentrate on getting well. This money came from a woman whose humble beginnings began as an orphan in rural Brazil. Ironically, Helder would have done anything to be able to go back to work. He was just too sick. I brought the kids to visit, but Helder couldn't hug them. It was a very sad and strained time for us. We were unaccustomed to sadness. It was an unfamiliar emotion for us. Helder could not be at the home he had built and so loved, and he had to stay away from his children, whom he cherished. Those were the sacrifices he had to make for the sake of beating this disease.

Helder was extremely lonely. It was one of the lowest points in his cancer battle, because he could not do any of the activities he enjoyed or be with the people he loved. During this time, he came to the realization he did not want to spend what might be the end of his life miserable in the small hope of looking for a cure. He would rather enjoy what time he had left. That was in 2007.

When Helder came home, Ester sent her church friends to the house to pray over Helder. Jose's friends came over, made a circle around his bed, and asked him if he accepted Jesus in his heart. "Why of course I do!" he proclaimed. Helder was a willing participant in the spiritual world. By the end of 2007, he had a clear scan. He was NED (no evidence of disease). Hallelujah!

2008 was the year without cancer. He had his portacath removed from his chest. In the early spring, Helder joined Tristan's Boy Scout troop and went camping at Camp Silver Fir.

They had to hike in on snow shoes. Helder felt good – really good. I had been a little concerned how he would do all of this with a colostomy, but you would never know he had one. He went back to work, coached Rebecca's, Tristan's and Rachel's soccer teams. When Jennifer went off to college, her dad was able to move her into her new dorm. For Tristan's twelfth birthday in February, Helder took him and his friends to play paintball. I asked Tristan afterwards how Dad did, and he said, "Oh Mom, he takes it so seriously! He was on the ground doing the GI Joe crawl, giving combat hand signals, and screaming to his teammates to duck down!" Helder was back to his old self again.

In November of that year, we received a phone call that Ester had suffered a massive stroke. We went to the hospital and she was already on a ventilator. The doctors told us she had bled into her brain. Although the bleeding had stopped, she would have permanent brain damage if she were to recover. They said it would be best to take her off the ventilator. Helder did not want to do anything until he found her advance directive document. He needed to see in writing if she wanted to prolong her life even if it meant having brain damage. It was important to him that each person's end-of-life wishes were respected. Once he recovered the paperwork, we scheduled the removal of the ventilator. Helder, Jennifer and I held hands as we watched Ester Viana pass away peacefully on November 16, 2008.

When we came home, we noticed there was a message on the answering machine. With all the hospital commotion, we hadn't paid attention to the machine. The message was left the morning of the stroke. She said, in her beautifully broken English with heavy Portuguese accent, "Helder, call me. It's your mother. I need to talk to you about your father. You must take care of him. He's old now and he needs you." Those were the last words he heard from his mother.

To say it was a big loss for Helder is an understatement. They had been through so much together, and she was the one constant in his life, throughout his parents' divorce, his brother's death and now, his own fight with cancer. She loved his children and he loved her even more for that. She came to every dance recital and school talent show. Helder took his mother practically everywhere with him, from trips to Hawaii to camping in Yosemite. He had been his mother's confidante and only living child. He also attributed his successes with fighting cancer to his mother's early spiritual intervention. Sometimes when he had no faith left, he leaned on hers. She always told us, "You have to pray like you really mean it." Ester had bought and paid for her own funeral expenses, including her casket. When we saw the one she had picked out, a plain pine casket, Helder laughed out loud. Then he cried. Although his mother had finally been financially comfortable, she still lived as if she were an orphan in South America.

Helder assumed the funeral arrangements would be simple, but here was the snag: Ester's second husband, Louie Sahfran, was Jewish. They were married for over 15 years. Louie had decided to purchase burial plots for both him and Ester in Mount Sinai, a Jewish cemetery. After Louie passed away, she married a man from the Adventist congregation, Oscar Fonseca. Interestingly, she didn't seem to care what religion her spouses were as long as they had one. This was a philosophy carried down to her son and passed on to his children. He always said,

"It doesn't matter who you believe in, Buddha, Jesus or God, but believe in a higher power." Helder and I sat in the office at Mount Sinai, listening to the funeral director go over arrangements when he asked if we would like their Rabbi to perform the services, or if we had one of our own. Helder and I looked at each other, blinked and looked back at the man. Helder was still very distraught and I sensed, although uncharacteristic, he didn't know what to say. After several awkward moments, I told the funeral director that Ester had been very involved in her church and someone from there would surely perform services. That's when we caught him by surprise, and he informed us, this was a Jewish cemetery (we didn't know), and it was Jewish law that no mention of Jesus could be included in the eulogy. There could be no cross or any references to Christianity on the gravestone. Helder and I held hands and we agreed. He had no intention of changing the arrangements his mother had previously made, even if those arrangements were with her now-deceased second husband. It all worked out because the minister was Brazilian and performed the service in Portuguese. No one could understand what was being said anyway.

That year we celebrated New Years' Eve in Las Vegas, so we could see the spectacular fireworks. We took Jose with us, and that's when we noticed he was having difficulty with his memory and thinking clearly. In early 2009, he was diagnosed with Alzheimer's disease. He was unable to renew his driver's license and had to use public transportation. One day Jose called Helder and asked him to come over because his television wasn't working. Helder arrived to find his father with his cordless telephone in his hand trying to turn on the TV. That wouldn't be so bad, except when Helder tried to explain to his dad that he was holding the telephone, Jose became agitated and insisted it was the TV remote. Eventually, we moved him into our guest room so we could take care of him. While it was difficult for Jose to let go of control over that part of his life, Helder was patient and understanding. He understood that his dad was a man who had had to fend for himself all his life. Jose never depended on anyone else, therefore it was a difficult transition for him to depend on his son. Helder packed up his father's belongings and put them in our garage. He transferred his telephone line to our house, so Jose could keep the same number. Helder took care of his dad just as his mother had asked him to.

Then in March, Helder's CEA level started rising. He had a scan and it showed a good sized spot on his lung. Coupled with increasing antigen levels, the spot was diagnosed as metastatic cancer.

Chapter Seven
Running Out of Options

Each time the cancer metastasized to a new area, there was a new office to visit; a new surgical specialist and office staff for Helder to get to know. He was referred to a thoracic surgeon this time. After the doctor reviewed the scans, he told us there was a tumor in Helder's lung, and he saw no problem in removing it. He described the excision in terms of a type of golf shot, "Like a chip shot," he very matter-of-factly told us. Helder had a laugh about that afterwards. I asked if there would be post-surgery chemotherapy. That's when the doctor said, "I'm counting on a cure here." That sounded good. We could use a cure!

Once again, we broke the news to the family. "Again?" was the response. Helder was very happy there was no chemotherapy in his future. The surgery was scheduled, and it felt like going through a familiar drill. Except this time, Jose was living with us. Helder asked me not to talk about his upcoming surgery unless someone asked. Our smaller circle of friends were told, but Helder said he was starting to feel like an oddity.

In the waiting room, I got the good news. The doctor reported a clear margin all the way around. The biopsy only tested positive for colorectal cancer. We considered it good news since some people get struck by lightning twice and end up with lung cancer *in addition to* colorectal cancer.

Life went back to normal that year. We had soccer games on the weekends, camping trips during the summer, dirt bike riding in the fall. There was even a ski trip to Utah in the winter. Helder even enjoyed wakeboarding on one of the summer camping trips.

Jennifer was on the honor roll at her college; Rebecca continued dance lessons and competitions; Tristan started high school and joined the soccer team, and Rachel joined the California Rangers, an equestrian drill team.

In 2010, Helder celebrated his forty-eighth birthday. That year Tristan began inviting five of his closest friends to go camping with us. They quickly became an integral part of our regular camping crew. Jennifer turned twenty-one that year, and Helder proudly lent her, and five of *her* closest friends, our SUV to take to Las Vegas to celebrate. Rebecca's soccer team was invited to play in the AYSO National Games, and she flew with her dad to Florida to play in the tournament. Rachel continued with her drill team and played her fifth year of soccer.

Then, in the latter part of that year, Helder's CEA level rose yet again. Another scan revealed a tumor; this time it was on his other lung, behind a rib. The thoracic surgeon, Dr. Roberts, said he would have to remove a section of the rib to get to the tumor. Again, Helder asked us not to publicize the surgery. It was discouraging to explain again and again the cancer was back, and he was doing all he could. Besides, he didn't want to be defined by his disease. He wanted to be treated like a regular Joe, not a cancer patient.

In our own little world, we had pockets of forgetting about cancer. If Helder was coaching a soccer game, or playing a video game, for that time he could almost forget the physical shape he was in. As it was, he ran across so many people who cared so deeply, and in that caring offered him many different cures. People left mangosteen juice, herbs,(both legal and illegal), and all sorts of other remedies which promised to cure cancer, on our doorstep. The outpouring of love was almost overwhelming. Helder confided that he was starting to feel like he was letting everyone down, especially his children.

Surgery was scheduled for November 10th. Dr. Roberts came to the waiting room and said his team was able to get the tumor; but once he removed the rib section, he found another tumor emanating from the rib. I didn't hear much after that. Helder's oncologist came to check in on him and told me he would need to have post-surgery chemotherapy. I sensed this was bad news. At the post-surgical checkup, the doctor told us there had been no clear margin, and there were most likely more cancer cells in the lung and rib area. He also said he would not go back inside to remove any additional cancer. At this point, a rigorous chemotherapy regime was the best way to treat Helder.

"How long will I need to be on chemotherapy?" Helder asked, almost timidly.

The doctor answered, "Probably for the rest of your life. You'll go for several weeks, then take a break, and continue for several more weeks."

Helder could not fathom taking chemotherapy for the rest of his life. Then we asked ourselves, "How long is that?" It might be shorter than we think.

Slowly Helder's CEA level started rising again. We went to get a second opinion from another oncologist as to how to proceed. I discussed which combination of chemotherapies Helder would probably need to take for the best outcome. I brought my file and went over all the ones he had previously been on. Suddenly the doctor interrupted me, "I know you might fire me for saying this, but I must tell you, eventually your husband's going to die from this cancer." As shocking as it was to hear, it was exactly what I needed. She saw that I was trying to figure out the magical combination of chemotherapies to *cure* Helder. I had become obsessed with figuring out survival percentages, and I'm sure I looked a little crazy. Although intellectually I knew chemotherapy does not cure metastatic cancer, clearly, I was in some sort of denial. Unfortunately, Helder was just following my lead. No one had told us he had moved into this new prognosis.

I have found doctors are generally uncomfortable when it comes to giving a prognosis. Some believe it's best not to give the patient too much information. The fact that she had to tell me, in front of Helder, tells me she felt compelled to give us the truth.

After we left the office, Helder told me what he does every time the cancer metastasized to another area, "I'm so sorry this is happening." In the midst of coming face to face with his own mortality, he had become profoundly spiritual, genuinely thinking of others before himself. He never asked, "Why is this happening to me?" Instead, he was pained by why this was happening to his loved ones. Helder was given the worst news over and over again, and his concern for his loved ones only got deeper.

In 2011, Helder joined a support group, Cancer Support Community, (CSC) in Pasadena. He first heard of it through a business contact, Catherine B., a few years before. Helder's cancer battle had come up during their initial meeting. She had suggested that a support group could be beneficial. Later, at a doctor's appointment for his father, a woman overheard his phone call with the surgeon's office. She said she was so sorry he had cancer and was still taking care of his father. She also suggested the CSC, which was funded by donors, and members did not have to pay for the services. After the second suggestion of a support group, Helder believed a divine power was urging him to attend. He stopped by the CSC office and came home with a pile of brochures, newsletters and an application which he promptly dropped on my desk and asked, "Could you find out what I need to do to get started with this? I think I need to be there." I took that to be a call for help. Being on the cancer roller coaster, Helder didn't talk much about his feelings. Going from the talk of cures with surgery then landing into chemo-therapy-for-life strategy was getting to him. While he never felt sorry for himself, that didn't mean he wasn't scared.

Helder connected with other members in the group almost immediately. He finally had a place to go to share his fears, his anger, and his never-ending optimism. I believe he could feel our relationship was wearing thin. I had to pick up the pieces in a lot of areas, and he didn't like it. He had always been the captain of our ship, and now he needed help steering. Helder was at a point where he was willing to surrender to his disease, knowing he had endured a lot of pain and suffering. He had begun to have his doubts, but he always concluded, "I'm not giving up."

This support group gave Helder a new extended family. Helder invited his new family to our annual Thanksgiving Open House. He participated in the group with a passion, the same passion he brought to everything he did. Helder suggested meeting for dinner after the group sessions. They also attended funerals together. One day he was asked by the administrator if CSC could feature him in a newsletter that was put out to commend its success. The following year, he was asked to speak at the annual board of directors' meeting where donor members were invited. His was a success story in that Helder had learned to really live with cancer.

Eventually we went to yet another oncologist who recommended a pill form of chemotherapy called Xeloda. Prior to this, Helder's chemo treatment was the standard FOLFOX, a cocktail of 5FU, leucovorin, and oxaliplatin. By using the pill form of chemo treatment, there was no need of a portacath, making life easier for him.

Helder started this new treatment. After four weeks, his blood work was done to check the CEA level. It had doubled, which had never happened before. Usually it was a slow rise. The doctor said not to worry because sometimes it takes a while to respond to this type of chemotherapy. In the meantime, the treatment caused nausea, so Helder's activities were limited.

Helder would watch Tristan's team play soccer in the afternoon. On several occasions, I watched him walk down to the bathroom to vomit, and then try to watch some more of the game. Another four weeks later the CEA level doubled yet again. The normal CEA level is below five. His was in the hundreds. Helder stopped the Xeloda and we went back to his primary care physician. The three of us brainstormed ideas. Helder said he didn't understand why surgery wasn't an option. After all, it only made sense, if they didn't get a clear margin to go back in and take another resection. He couldn't accept that surgery was not a possibility, especially since with surgery there is a possible cure, and it increases the odds of prolonging life.

Eventually his doctor found a thoracic surgeon affiliated with the University of Southern California. She was able to get a referral after providing documentation. While it was difficult to get a referral to a doctor outside the network with an HMO, it was not impossible. A scan was taken of his chest wall and ribs. We then scheduled a meeting with the new surgeon.

We waited nervously while the surgeon reviewed the PET scan. Finally, he brought us into his very large office – not an exam room. There were two assistant surgeons with him. He said "I can see the tumor in your chest wall causing the rise in CEA, there is also tumor activity on your rib and surrounding tissue. I think I can remove a section of your rib, as well as a section of your chest wall." There was a pause while the doctors waited for a response, and then Helder jumped up, "Well, that's good news!" There was dead silence from the surgeons. "Well, come around here and let's look at this "good news" on the screen and discuss some details," the main doctor replied. Apparently, they had never seen a stage IV cancer patient jump for joy at the suggestion of a complicated surgery. When I retold the story to his primary physician, she explained that Helder had an unusually optimistic attitude which most cancer doctors do not often see.

Surgery was scheduled for April 14, 2012. At this point, Helder was only working part-time which meant only when previous customers called. He stopped advertising all together.

After the surgery, Dr. Robbins came into the waiting room to tell me it was a success. In addition to the tumor, and resection of the fifth rib, a large margin was removed, and it was taken to the lab while he was still on the operating table. The results were a clear margin all the way around. This time, however, Helder had a difficult time with the recovery. Fluid had gotten into his lungs, and after a few days at home, he had to go back to the hospital.

I was with Rebecca and Rachel at Huntington Memorial Hospital, when the nurses asked us to wait outside while the doctor performed an emergency drain. While we were waiting, I heard Helder cry out in pain, and I quickly walked the girls to the nearest waiting room where there was a door I could close. Later, I learned he received only a local anesthesia before an incision was made next to his rib for inserting a drainage tube.

Four months after the surgery, a new scan revealed multiple tumors in both lungs. I called the surgeon as soon as I received a copy of the report. He said that there must be a mistake. Another scan was taken, and we met with the surgeon, this time in a small examination room without his assistants. The only thing he could do was refer us back to an oncologist for chemotherapy to prolong Helder's life. My husband asked him why he couldn't go in again and remove the new tumors. The doctor explained there was a high probability that there would be more tumors which they could not see yet, that it would not be in a patient's best interest to continue to perform surgery when it keeps spreading. He went on to explain if the tumors were all in one lung, it might be an option. Operating on both lungs was not an option. Helder told him, "If you wanted to you could do the surgery," and walked out of the room. It was the first time he felt defeated.

Chapter Eight
Chemo for Life

Jose had been attending an adult day care that sent a van to the house to pick him up Monday through Friday; but in 2012, it became apparent he needed around the clock care care. The dementia, a side effect of Alzheimer's, was compromising his ability to reason and make judgments. We were told by his psychiatrist that without constant care, he could easily open the front door at night while we were sleeping and walk out of our house. During the day, it was just as difficult because I worked full-time, and Helder's health issues prevented him from being as attentive as he wanted to be with his father. He struggled with the decision, but one day he got up from a nap, and found his dad urinating on the tree in our front yard. When Helder told him that was inappropriate behavior, he argued it was his right to urinate wherever he wanted. We knew we needed to find a place that would love and care for Jose. We shopped around and fell in love with a family-owned retirement home that had been in business since 1990.

At first, we started off slow and told Jose we were going away for the weekend, and he was staying there temporarily. He didn't understand why he had to stay there. Helder did his best at encouraging him by telling him it was a privilege to live there. They served meals in a dining hall where he could talk with other residents; he could participate in the daily activities such as dancing, stretching, and other senior home activities.

Helder went to visit him every day. He took him for a walk to the nearby park and would bring a nail clipper, so he could clip his fingernails while they sat on the park bench. Other times, he brought a hair trimmer and would cut his hair and give him a shave. Months later, Jose started talking gibberish, but he always recognized Helder and would give him a soft kiss on the cheek. Helder put together a small shrine of pictures on a shelf in his room: one of his father at the Seventh Day Adventist boarding school, a photo of him in his soccer uniform, and pictures with his grandchildren. At the end of the year, Helder asked his children if they would join him in singing Christmas carols at the retirement home. They all invited friends, and we had about a dozen of us singing carols that year. When Helder's health started to deteriorate, he went twice a week and then weekly. Throughout his battle with cancer, he always visited his father, took him for a walk, and cut his hair and his fingernails. He felt it was a show of love to take care of his father's hygiene, knowing how important cleanliness was to him.

Helder needed to have the portacath re-inserted to start chemotherapy. At first, he delayed it while he struggled with the idea of doing chemotherapy for life. He also struggled with living with cancer in his body. For the last eight years, he had been on a mission to uncover and discard any cancer in his body. The result was always to cure the cancer he had. Changing the eventual outcome of his treatment plan from curing the disease to learning to live with cancer was a smack in the face for Helder. He had been told so many times they were expecting a cure; it was difficult to accept there was not going to be one.

During this time, Helder was understandably depressed. Nevertheless, he always found something inspirational to keep him motivated and positive. The cancer support group played an important role in helping him keep his spirits up. It gave him a place to openly share the dark feelings that would come up, and how he felt discouraged at times. It was a place to talk about the loneliness he felt having cancer. He could voice the anger he felt about cancer robbing him from a future he would never have with his children or the grandchildren he had hoped to have one day. Sometimes Helder felt no one could quite understood him like others living with cancer. He felt truly blessed in finding the support group, and the love and acceptance he received from the members and staff. He loved laughing with the other members about the ironies of living with cancer. He shared one of them with me, which happens when breaking the bad news to a friend about having cancer. A common response is, "But you look so good!" The irony of dying while still "looking good" was not lost on Helder and his friends from the support group. They had their inappropriate jokes about death, which only they could understand as funny. They were sensitive to the fact that loved ones wouldn't find them funny.

The hardest thing for Helder was accepting that he had multiple tumors in both his lungs, and the best he could hope for was to prolong his life by continuing chemotherapy treatment indefinitely. It was a very strange time for us. Helder had to wake up every day to cancer, with no plan for a cure. Once he came to terms with the treatment plan, we scheduled the outpatient surgery to have a portacath re-inserted into his chest. Soon after, the area became infected. Helder was referred to a wound care specialist to treat the infection. All of this took time, so he was unable to start chemotherapy until January of 2013. To help all of us cope with this, we rented a cabin at Big Bear Lake. Helder rented skis and went down an easy trail one time. Then he announced he was hungry and it was lunch time. That was the last time he skied.

The reality of cancer would always find us. His oncologist suggested a stronger regimen which included Irinotecan. The side effects of this drug caused neuropathy in his hands and feet. Helder said the neuropathy in his feet felt like someone was taking a baseball bat and beating the bottoms of his feet. Eventually, the neuropathy affected his ability to bend his fingers without feeling horrible pain. Helder endured this pain for a year.

He requested Monday as his weekly infusion day, so he could recover from the nausea by the weekend and be available to coach his soccer games on Saturday, while playing soccer himself on Sunday. The nausea was awful; and although he gradually felt better by the end of the week, it was only to start over again on Monday. After several months of this, Helder decided to have one good week for every one lost week. He changed his treatments to bi-weekly, so he had more time with his family, doing the things he enjoyed in life. He soon began weighing the quality of his life versus prolonging his life. He began to question cancer treatments if it meant shortening the quality of time he had left.

In 2013, Tristan registered to become a referee with the United States Soccer Federation to earn extra money refereeing club youth games. It was his first job as a teenager. Helder also registered so they could referee together. Tristan was getting ready to apply to colleges and would soon be flying the coop the following year.

During this phase of "chemo for life" treatment program, Helder was keenly aware of his mortality, and the catch phrase he often used was, "This could be the last time." Or, "Next year I might not be here to..." Although it sounded morbid, after a while the reality of those thoughts encouraged Helder to try things he may have given up on and pushed himself to participate. When things got tough, he got tougher. Helder was worried his health would compromise his ability to referee, but again he pushed through it, allowing him and Tristan to referee several games together throughout the year. Eventually, his health made it difficult to continue, so he found a used car for Tristan, so he could go out on his own.

That year, Helder bought new dirt bikes for the family. He wanted to share his love for dirt bike riding with the family. Sometimes he and Tristan would go on their own because they were more skilled at riding the more difficult runs. On one of these trips, Helder had gone up a steep hill, not knowing what he would find once he went over. Unfortunately, there was no plateau, and what he found on the other side was a steep downhill slope. He started going too fast and lost control of the bike. The way he told the story, he "luckily" hit a large rock which stopped the bike, resulting in him flying over the handlebars and landing on dirt. Tristan had to help him walk the bike back up the hill and eventually back to the truck. Helder was in a lot of pain that night, mostly in his rib area.

The next morning, I took him to an urgent care clinic. While we were waiting for the doctor, I told him, "You have to be more careful, Helder. After all the surgeries and chemotherapy treatments, wouldn't it be ironic if you died from a dirt bike riding accident?" (Helder and I didn't talk much about cancer in those days. The bi-weekly chemotherapy treatments were all we would allow to invade our lives. It was an unspoken agreement not to bring it up, especially on the weeks he didn't have chemo.) Helder paused for several moments and replied, "I don't want to die lying in a bed with my family watching me suffer to take my last breaths. What would be a better way to go than being out in nature doing what I love." I walked over to him and gave him a long hug and kissed his face a hundred times. He wasn't going to let cancer win.

That Fall, Helder had blood work done to see if he was responding to the chemotherapy treatment. The results showed the CEA was rising. Helder was so sick and tired of being sick and tired from the chemo, he was quick to declare, "Well, that didn't work!" The question then was how much would the CEA have risen if he had not undergone nine months of chemotherapy. When you're in that stage of cancer, you quickly realize it's a guessing game. It's frightening when you realize medicine is not an exact science. There are so many factors involved. Expected results are given in percentages and five-year survival rates. No one was willing to guess what the odds were for Helder at that point. His oncologist told him he was a miracle of modern medicine. Although it had been nine years since he had first been diagnosed, he wasn't giving up. Helder eventually became his doctor's longest living patient with stage IV cancer.

Helder asked for a referral for another surgeon to get a second opinion. He wanted to see if some of the larger tumors could be removed, giving him more time. It was his opinion surgery always worked well for him. Knowing there was a surgery option meant there was hope.

His lungs were scanned, and an appointment was scheduled for December 17th. We sat in the surgeon's office while he reviewed the scan on the monitor. He spoke out loud, listing where all the tumors were located – some in the interior portion of the lung, one particularly large one on the top side of the lung by the airway, several in the membrane between the chest wall and the lung, and quite a few in the deep tissue of the lung itself. After a good amount of time, the doctor asked, "So why are you here today?" Helder said he was hoping some of the larger tumors could be removed. Then the doctor carefully responded, "Since you have tumors in both your lungs, and in various sections of your lungs, surgery is not an option for you." Helder quickly said, "Why couldn't you remove the ones you *can* get to, and not focus on the ones you *cannot* get to?" Helder was always the optimist. He prayed, "God grant me the serenity to accept the things I cannot change, the courage to change the things I can, and the wisdom to know the difference." The surgeon replied, "There are always risks to surgery. To look at you, you seem to be doing well. You appear physically well. Your scan tells a different story and most certainly does not match what I'm seeing sitting in that chair. A surgeon must weigh out the risks versus the outcome. The risk of performing surgery on your lungs far outweighs a positive outcome of this proposed surgery. Removing those tumors which I can get to will not prolong your life, because I would be leaving behind large tumors in almost every section of your lung." That's when Helder asked him, "Is it because your reputation is on the line? Are you concerned it might not look good if you perform this surgery, and still leave tumors behind?" The surgeon said, "I don't know of any surgeon who would perform such an operation. The risk is too high, the outcome too poor." They went back and forth like this for a while. Finally, the doctor said, "What I can do is submit your case to the USC Cancer Board (a committee of surgeons, doctors and oncologists who review cases), see what their opinions are, and I will get back to you." Helder agreed, got up and walked out the door and didn't stop until he got to the car.

I was left apologizing for his abrupt exit. I know Helder felt defeated, and he had come to the realization this might be the beginning of the end. He had said from the beginning he did not want to chase the cure. He knew plenty of people who had gone to Mexico to look for a cure, only to return on death's bed, having wasted that precious time away from their loved ones. More importantly for him, he didn't want to feel desperate. He wanted to let go while he still had the dignity and self-respect he had regained in sobriety. Helder always remained grateful and knew he had lived a good life. He had experienced a miraculous intervention diverting him from the path of destruction, to the wonderful family life he had always longed to have. Being in that surgeon's office took him right to the doorstep of desperation. I could feel it, and he could feel it. He never went there again. Helder made a conscious decision to accept the things he could not change. He wanted to live the rest of his life with serenity and peace, which was good, because the surgeon never got back to him.

Next, Helder wanted to obtain an opinion from his previous doctor at City of Hope. Since it was considered one of the most innovative and groundbreaking centers for cancer research, treatment and recovery, he felt like it would be due diligence to have the doctors there weigh in on his current situation. We went to visit Dr. L. later that month.

Dr. L. went over the recent scans and confirmed that the chemo treatment Helder had been doing that year was precisely what he would have recommended. He mentioned a new trial for a drug that basically retards the growth of the cancer cells, allowing late stage cancer patients to prolong their life. Helder asked, "Are there any side effects, and how much additional time would it give me?" which only a well-seasoned cancer patient would know to ask. Dr. L. responded, "This is the first stage of the trial. Some of the patients will be given a placebo, and some the actual medicine. You will not know. The side effect we have seen is blindness, however; it's a very small percentage. But it will give you anywhere from one to three months longer than if you did not take it." Helder and I slowly looked at each other, eye to eye, for a reality check. Were we hearing correctly? Helder blurted out, "There are people willing to risk blindness and nausea for *possibly* one more month of life?" Dr. L. said, "Yes, quite a few. For some people that one month is everything." Helder said, "Not if you're blind and sick for that one month, when you could possibly have a few weeks of just feeling good with your family." Dr. L. said he should think about it and proceeded with a physical exam.

When Dr. L. examined Helder's body, he gasped. Helder had surgical battle scars criss-crossing the middle of his chest down to his pelvic area, deep scars on the sides, some to access the liver, some to access the lungs and some to access the ribs. He also had large scars on his chest from implanting and removing the porta-cath. When asked if he was experiencing any pain, Helder said he could feel a dull pain in his lungs when he took a deep breath, but that was it. Although he had bouts of extreme fatigue, his lifestyle allowed him to take regular naps in the afternoon. "Other than cancer, I'm feeling great, Doc!" Helder joked.

The nerve damage in Helder's hand, a side effect of the chemotherapy, had not dissipated, so Helder made an appointment to see a hand surgeon. After x-rays were taken, two surgeries were scheduled, one hand at a time. After physical therapy, Helder regained the strength and use of his hands.

Chapter Nine
Living with Cancer

In the Fall of 2013, Rachel, then in the 8th grade, started a new school, Heritage Christian School. She chose this school because a good friend of hers had left public school for a Christian-based institution, and she felt like it would be a good fit for her as well. Helder thought it ironic his parents had subjected him to religious schools growing up, some of which he ran away from, and now his daughter was asking to go to one. At the same time, Helder had begun to warm up to organized religion, although he still felt some of the pangs of emotional hurt he endured as a child stemming from a punitive religious upbringing. Nevertheless, it was hard for him to turn down his daughter wanting to go to a Christian-based school.

Helder, always social, introduced himself to some of the parents and met Frank, who told him HCS had a girls' soccer team. Helder told him Rachel had been playing soccer for most her life and she would try out for the team. He also told Frank he had coached her all those years, along with his other kids for many years in the AYSO soccer league. As it turns out, the school was looking for a coach, and Frank thought Helder would be a perfect match. Although he barely knew Helder, he felt inspired by his enthusiasm for soccer, and took it upon himself to advocate for Helder to get the job. After a series of events, he was hired to coach the girls' soccer team at Heritage Christian School. For Helder, the timing was perfect. He was done with "chemo for life" and he wanted to live a normal lifestyle with his family. His carpet cleaning days had petered out for the most part. He was ecstatic to be hired for the position. It was a dream come true for him. He had only wished his mother was still alive to see him coaching soccer at a Christian school. She would have been thrilled, to say the least.

As part of the application process, Helder had to submit to a background check, verifying the information on his application. It takes several weeks to get the results of the Live Scan. In his mind, the trouble he got into when he was younger (over twenty-five years ago) was of the "non-felony" variety and didn't mention it on his application. Besides, he had thought, it happened over twenty-five years ago, mostly when he was a minor. Also, another side effect of chemotherapy is confusion and memory loss. "Chemo brain" is how it's affectionately referred to among cancer patients. Sadly, it's a very real side effect of long term chemotherapy. Early dementia can also set in, and confusion about facts, memory loss, and the inability to complete tasks becomes a normal state of being. That had been happening gradually to Helder. When it came time to complete the application, he couldn't remember times and dates very well and completed it as best as he could. I told him I couldn't help because that all happened BC "Before Carol".

Helder started after-school practices right away in January of 2014. If 2013 was the year of chemo, then 2014 was the year of living. Helder voiced his concern about what would happen if the cancer suddenly worsened or if the dull pain in his lungs became sharper, or if his breathing became affected. He didn't want to drop out in the middle of the season, leaving the girls with no coach. He wrestled with it for a short while. If there ever was a cancer wish list, this was on Helder's. He felt God granted his wish.

Helder soon discovered he was expected to pray with the team before every practice and every game. After finding this out, he came home a little stressed. He had never prayed before a game with his numerous other teams and thought it might feel awkward. He confessed he wasn't quite at that level of daily spiritual practice. Being a creative man, on the first day of practice, Helder asked for a volunteer. Helder told me the girl who volunteered said her own prayer, asking our Heavenly Father to bless the team, bless their new coach, and keep everyone safe while practicing. It was done with such confidence and sincerity, Helder was touched by the experience. He also said it went so well, he made asking for a volunteer a regular part of practice. He felt this prayer ritual was an unexpected perk of his new position. He told me, "How fortunate am I, every time I go to work, I get to pray with fellow Christians?"

One day Helder received a call from the school's administration, asking to set up a meeting with him. He was immediately nervous and suspicious. "Why would they want to meet with me?" he kept asking. He wondered if he had said or done something wrong during practice. Did his references not check out? Finally, he went in for the meeting, and there in the conference room were the Director of the Athletic department, the director of the school, and the school office manager. One of the directors asked, "We received your Live Scan back and there is a felony charge listed from 1985 for possession and intent to sell marijuana. Can you explain?" Helder paused a moment and did what he had been doing for the past twenty-four years when asked to share about his recovery. He shared his experience, strength and hope, and proceeded to tell them, in a general way, what it used to be like, what happened, and what it was currently like for him. That was all he could think of doing – revert to what he knows best. Helder paused a moment and did what he had been doing for the past twenty-four years when asked to share about his recovery. He shared his experience of strength and hope, and proceeded to tell them, in a general way, what it used to be like, what happened, and what it was currently like for him. That was all he could think of doing – to revert to doing what he knows best. As was always the case when he told his story, he had them laughing, he brought them to tears, and he left them in awe of what he accomplished purely by the grace of God.

After that hurdle, Helder felt right at home. He got to know the parents, and they got to know him. He asked me to coordinate weekly dinners, one or two days before a game, so the team could have some bonding time. This is what the high school soccer teams did, and he incorporated it into his soccer program. The families loved it, and soon Helder transmitted his infectious soccer energy to his new soccer family. At first it looked like just another year of middle school soccer to the parents, but what they didn't know was that he was planning on winning the league championship. The first few games were no indication this would ever happen. After a while, and with his non-stop positive energy working with the girls, getting some of them to score goals for their very first time, the team started winning. Their team ended the season in first place. It was a proud moment for Helder. It was the first time he was paid for coaching soccer. He enjoyed being a part of a Christian school, and it was extremely fulfilling to be able to teach the girls the soccer skills he had learned throughout the years.

That spring, we planned a camping trip with the Lamm family, our neighbor Linda Miller and her son, a close friend of Tristan, a few of their mutual friends, and our daughters Jennifer and Rachel. We were about fourteen people, and Helder cooked dinner for us all. He also brought Guarana, a Brazilian soda made with the guarana fruit, to share with everyone. When Helder was growing up, Guarana soda was served whenever there was a family celebration. He knew his camping days were running out, so he went all out; he bought two wave runners, so everyone could take turns riding them on the lake when we weren't on the boat. Helder loved "hosting" a camp out, providing dinner and all the necessary camping equipment. It was one of his favorite things to do.

His health was slowly declining. Breathing was becoming more difficult; he couldn't take a full deep breath anymore. Initially it scared him, and brought a little anxiety, but he just learned to pace himself. Helder had heard there was a new kind of chemotherapy, called targeted chemotherapy. If successful, it would slow down the tumor growth.

Helder made an appointment to see another surgical oncologist who we will call Dr. P. This required another lung scan. At this point, Helder could no longer endure a full body scan without taking a sedative. Something in his mind had snapped, and the anxiety it caused was overwhelming. After Dr. P. looked at the scan, he turned to Helder and asked, head tilted to one side, "So what brings you here today?" Helder replied, with a smile, "I was wondering if surgery was an option?" At first Dr. P. looked worried, even scared, but then he saw Helder's grin, they both laughed. My heart went out to Helder. He was at that place where he had to find the humor because his situation had gotten so sad. He proceeded to ask the surgeon about the new targeted chemotherapy he had heard about on public radio. Dr. P. had to refer him to a medical oncologist, he was a surgeon and wasn't sure why the referral was made for him. They said good-bye and Dr. P. wished Helder best of luck, neither one of them knowing their paths would cross again.

Tristan graduated high school in June of 2014 and was admitted to California State University, better known as "Chico State", majoring in computer science. Helder flew to Chico for Parent Appreciation Day, and proudly moved Tristan into his new dorm.

In the Fall of that year, AYSO soccer began and Helder was asked if he could coach a boys' U10 team. Boys under ten-years-old are the largest group of players, and our region didn't have enough volunteers to coach. Most people in his life were unaware of the extent of his cancer. He liked it that way, because he was treated no differently.

Helder agreed to coach the younger players, since he only had Rachel's team to coach instead of the usual two, sometimes three teams. His three older kids were away at college. He suggested Rachel be his assistant coach, which meant she had to be trained as a referee as well. That season she was blessed with coaching alongside her dad. The players' parents could hardly believe Helder was coaching a team without one of his children on it, *and* his fourteen-year-old daughter wanted to be his assistant coach. Not to mention they were Brazilian! Helder loved having a ten-year-old audience once again. Sometimes it seemed he was more excited watching the boys play than their own parents. One more time, he put 150% of his energy into coaching.

At this point Helder started to cough. Despite the times he couldn't catch his breath, considering he wasn't on any treatment, he felt he was living a very good life. He was still able to coach soccer, see his son off to college and, at the end of that year, plan a trip to Europe, which included France and Italy. Helder often said, "Life is good!"

In spring of 2015, Helder learned of SB128, a bill being considered by Governor Jerry Brown called the End of Life Option Act. It would enable anyone who was terminally ill and had been diagnosed with six months or less to live, to be prescribed a lethal dose of sedatives to end their own life. It was not a physician-assisted act, rather a decision in which mentally capable terminal patients would have to administer the dose to themselves. Helder asked me to find out more about the bill and what it would take to get the medication. When the time came, he didn't want to drag out his death like his brother was forced to do, and so many others he had known through his cancer support group. He knew there was no way of knowing how a person with cancer would die. He didn't want to cause me or the children any more suffering and anguish, or have us watch him gasping for breath. Helder spent the last ten years at the mercy of his body with the disease spreading throughout his organs. He had no control over the surgeries, body scans, cleanses, or the nausea and brain fog from chemotherapy. His lungs had been drained, ribs removed, and he maintained an active life living with a colostomy. I told Helder he earned the right to decide when and how he died.

Helder lived a fairly normal life without chemo treatment, which lasted longer than he anticipated. He had been told chemotherapy would prolong his life; yet, no one was willing to predict how long that life would be. His doctors were amazed at how well he was doing with the number and size of tumors in his lungs. Without chemo he fully enjoyed the life he had. Eventually his health got progressively worse; most noticeably was the chronic fatigue. Nevertheless, a camping trip was planned for Memorial Day weekend in 2015. The trip to Buena Vista Lake was encouraged by our kids. I don't think Helder would have initiated one at this point, but he was easily persuaded. The kids brought their friends and their friends' parents, who were now our friends. Although most of the kids were already in college, it remained a sober camping trip, with Coca-Cola and Guarana soda being the strongest beverages served. It was a magical time for Helder, being Dad to so many, camping, cooking and reliving a little nostalgia of a time when his kids were much younger. He was sure it felt the same for them. They say you can't go back and be a child again, but he made it seem possible. We were a total of fourteen people on that trip. It was also Helder's last camping trip.

It was an unspoken understanding that these two years were precious, and the moments together should be treasured. When we were together we laughed a little harder, were more understanding than usual, and made the best of most situations. Helder said repeatedly that cancer had been a mixed blessing. It allowed him to appreciate his life in a way he may not have done without the threat of impending death. He was more accepting of his children's ups and downs, and less demanding of himself and others. Cancer took the edge off of living. Every day alive was a good day for Helder.

In November of 2015, Tristan came home from college and said he had something he wanted to share with us. We were out to dinner, just the three of us. Tristan proceeded to tell us he wanted to join the United States Marine Corps. He told us that if he passed certain tests, he could qualify for the Intelligence Division His background in computer science, along with his math skills, could qualify him for this battalion. Tristan outlined the reasons he wanted to enlist, one of which was he wanted to be a part of something bigger; he also wanted to learn self-discipline and have a purpose. Helder had not expected this. He hadn't realized how courageous and honorable his son was at the young age of nineteen. He shared with us that he, too, had wanted to join the USMC when he was nineteen. He had never told anyone until that moment, because of the shame he felt of not being accepted. He told us it was a dream of his, but he was turned down because he didn't have a high school diploma.

Helder was very proud his son would carry on what he wasn't able to do himself.

During that time, new blood work was taken, and a new scan was ordered. Helder's CEA level was well into the hundreds. We made an appointment with the City of Hope and the doctors there recommended a new FDA approved drug called Stivarga. It was specifically for patients with metastatic colorectal cancer which was no longer responding to traditional treatments. Helder asked what the outcome would be, and he was told it would add as much as four to six weeks to his life. We looked at each other with raised eyebrows. Neither one of us wanted to ask the dreaded question. When we came home, I wrote to Dr. L. and asked how much time he thought Helder had. He told us based on the size and number of tumors, without chemotherapy he would have probably three to six months, and with chemo, possibly another six months. That was in late December. Helder started talking about his funeral arrangements. He would talk about it at dinner. He would talk about it before we went to bed. We would go out to lunch and talk about it. It was important to him the kids have an occasion to speak if they wanted. He wanted to make a video, leaving a message behind for each one.

Helder was asked to speak at our regular Friday night AA meeting that year, and the secretary had not realized it fell on Christmas. He told Helder he didn't have to come out since it was the holiday, that he could speak the following month, but he felt compelled to come out on that night and so he did. He shared about his new prognosis. He also shared about his gratitude and the lessons he had learned living with cancer. Someone recorded him that evening, and here is an excerpt:

"From my first diagnosis, I did not see a gift or any miracles that came with cancer. It took time for the double-edged sword of destiny to reveal itself. The moment I realized I had a choice, or there were two sides to cancer, I decided to either start living with my diagnosis, or accept the horror of not being in control. I began my journey of self-awareness. I started asking questions; how can I become the best person I can be today? How do I become authentic, sincere and open with myself, my family and all the people I meet and have known? My first step was to begin living in the moment. I began to realize that right here, right now I am alive and I am capable of loving myself and others just the way I am. I started appreciating my life, and I know now I would not have had that appreciation if I didn't have cancer. I started appreciating every relationship, and would not have, had it not been for cancer. I visited places and took vacations I would not have, had I not had cancer. I learned how to stop hiding. I learned how to see myself as a beautiful, delicate flower. As often as possible."

On New Years' Eve 2015, Helder and I went to a sober event, complete with dancing and a disco ball. Tristan insisted on joining us, along with close friends, Brenton, Elika, Jesse and Ariel, who by now had a long history with Helder through countless camping trips. Rachel and her friend, Amber, also came along. We brought in the new year, dancing together. It was an odd feeling that evening, because the information was still so new. No one was talking about it, we all felt that it might be Helder's last New Year. He did not want to be defined by this new death sentence, yet at the same time he wanted to experience and appreciate every moment because of it.

One change became apparent. Helder, who could draw an audience with his quick wit and charm, who once held court at every gathering, no longer wanted to be the center of attention. He started to slowly withdraw. It was a very slow and very slight process, but it had begun.

Chapter Ten
Bucket List

Helder began talking about end-of-life decisions. He wanted to make sure our financial affairs were in order, which to him meant tightening our belts and paying down our mountain of accumulated debt. He became worried about the financial burden we would have to bear once he passed on. Finally, I had to tell him, "Helder, I'm pretty sure if I were in your shoes, there would be some last wishes I would want to fulfill. I am giving you permission to travel, to dine out, to buy front of the line passes, or whatever you desire. I say that without worry because I know you'll still be conservative in your desires, but really, *now* is the time. Even though you're having difficulty breathing, you can still get around. We don't know how long that's going to last." Helder looked at me dumbfounded. He had been so engulfed with thoughts about his own shame and guilt of leaving his family, he couldn't see beyond it. He could not imagine thinking of things he would like to do while he still could. I planned a trip every month: January was the Florida Keys; February was Belize with Tristan for his birthday before he left for boot camp, and March was Hawaii for Helder's 54th birthday.

Only Rebecca and Tristan were available to go with us to Florida, so the four of us rented a car and drove from Key Largo to Key West. First, we went snorkeling in a coral reef sanctuary. Helder was nervous about managing his breathing, especially if he should get one of his coughing attacks. As it turned out, he did just fine. During this trip, he kept reminding me he couldn't walk too far, and he needed to rest in the afternoon. I reassured him we could stop whenever he needed, and we kept the daily touristy trips light.

Belize was a different set of circumstances. Helder was talking about getting an Open Water Diving Certification, which enables you to dive at greater depths. Unlike the tourist certification, which is only good for a limited diving depth and expires once you leave the resort, an "open water" certification never expires. Helder had gone scuba diving twice before under a tourist certification and always wanted to be able to get "open water" certified, so he could go whenever he wanted. He also said, "It might be easier to breathe with oxygen tanks, after all, that's what I will eventually have to live with." The first part of certification is done in the swimming pool, so we agreed to see how he would do there, and then decide if he could complete the ocean portion. I arranged for Helder and Tristan to get scuba certified while diving in Belize. They did the written portion at home and were scheduled for the water portion when we arrived. Our hotel was right on the beach, and we took a small propeller plane from Belize City to the beach town of Dangriga. It rained most of the time we were there, yet with temperatures in the 80s (and 80% humidity) we kept our windows open, and took pleasure in the sound of the rain. Since the three of us enjoyed reading, and there was no TV in the room, we spent most of our time lying on our beds, reading. Helder's favorite author was Stephen King, and as it happened, each of us was reading a different Stephen King book. Helder had a compelling way of encouraging us to read his favorite books. We discussed the chapters we had read over our meals. It was a relaxing, magical time.

The first day of scuba lessons was spent practicing in the pool. Later that day Helder told me he was a little nervous about breathing below the surface in the ocean, but so far, he thought he would be all right. On the second day, Tristan and his dad went out on the scuba boat to where they could go through the remaining certification sequences. I had gone to get a massage, and when I came back, Tristan was on the dock and told me Dad went to the room. I knew something was wrong. Helder wouldn't have left so quickly without chatting with the instructors. When I got to the room, he told me, "I think I had a panic attack." He said he felt like he couldn't breathe, and he started to get very anxious. He had not gone under water, instead he had done certification exercises on the surface and that's when it began. The waves were choppy, and it made him feel like he might not be able to catch his breath. The instructor held on to Helder in a rescue position and got him safely back on the boat. Helder said he now understood how devastating panic attacks can be. He also told me the scuba instructor did something that stayed with him. As he was panicking out on the water, the instructor came behind him and told him to lie on his back. The instructor had his arms around Helder's shoulders and told him, "You're safe now. I'm holding you and you are safe here with me." Helder said those words calmed him and he could breathe normally again. Later that day he confessed to the instructor that he had numerous tumors in his lungs and thought he would be all right to get certified. The instructor said he would sign off on his certification, with one caveat – Helder would not be certified to go past a certain depth. Helder had no plan to actually go diving on this trip, nor in the future. After that, Helder remained subdued for the rest of the trip, and the fear of having another panic attack stayed with him for a while.

After we returned home, Helder's primary physician advised us that he was eligible for hospice care since he had received a prognosis of six months or less survival. I told Helder we could start interviewing hospice agencies, but he was not comfortable with being in hospice phase at that time. Then his doctor told us about palliative care, which is available to patients with serious and grave illnesses. The purpose of palliative care is to assure that the patient is comfortable and address relief of any symptoms. Helder knew he wanted to die at home, so we were looking for an in-home hospice/palliative care agency. When the agency nurses would arrive, one by one for interviewing, we would urgently ask if there was anything that could be done to assist Helder with his breathing. He was not eligible for oxygen yet, because his oxygen levels had to be below a certain level for insurance to cover it. He knew that a few drops of opiates would help with his breathing. The palliative care nurse explained that the properties of morphine, in the smallest dosage, cause the breathing to slow down. It was also suggested he start taking Ativan for anxiety, which was affecting his breathing as well. (Or was his breathing causing the anxiety? No one could answer that question. We would joke, it was quite the conundrum!) Helder preferred not to take either one, but after several sleepless nights having to sit upright in his recliner chair to sleep, he agreed to take a small dose of Ativan before bedtime.

In March, Rebecca was unable go to Hawaii because of school, so just the five of us went and stayed at a hotel on Kaanapali Beach. Helder was looking forward to this vacation because he thought the Hawaiian air would help him breathe easier. It was a wonderful place. Helder wanted Jennifer to scuba dive because she had never done it before. He also wanted Tristan to use his newly acquired scuba certification.

The dive was to take place in a nearby cove, so Helder was confident he would be all right in the water. As soon as they swam out about thirty feet from the shore, he started to panic again, and he swam back to shore. I was sitting on the beach waiting for them. I immediately saw how distraught he was. He was trembling and pale. All I could say was, "You're going to be all right. You're going to be okay." And soon he was. Helder never went in the ocean again after that.

When we returned home, he told me he was done with traveling. He just wanted to be home with his family – everyone together at the same time. We celebrated his fifty-fourth birthday on March 25th at a Brazilian steakhouse, followed by a birthday movie, *Batman vs Superman*, two of his favorite superheroes. One of the men who Helder sponsored in recovery worked in advertising and gave Helder a replicate of the movie poster. He continued to be thought of and loved by so many.

Helder continued going to his support group at the

Cancer Support Community. One night he told me that while he had been sitting in the meeting, he saw flashing lights in the corner of his eye. He initially thought it was from a ceiling fan making a reflection in his glasses. But when he looked up, there was no ceiling fan. We would later learn what was causing those flashing lights.

He brought home a book from his cancer support group called *The Dash*. The premise of the book is that when people die, the focus is on two dates, birth and death; instead we should focus on the dash in between. When Tristan received his notice that boot camp would start on April 24th, Helder realized he wanted to spend as much time as he could living in the dash, rather than focusing on the end date.

He made an appointment with Pastor Dave at Montrose Church to discuss his funeral arrangements. Helder had become very fond of Pastor Dave throughout the years. His church possessed just the right mix of dogma, historical facts, and spirituality to interest Helder but not so much that it would scare him away. He wanted to be there though he wasn't sure if he would be completely accepted. He had been baptized when he was thirteen and confirmed at thirty-two when we joined All Saints Episcopal Church in Pasadena where all four of our children were baptized.

Helder wanted to be cremated. There was absolutely no doubt. I tried to argue with him and told him there wouldn't be a place for us to go and visit with him. He responded, "My ashes, placed in the urn of your choice, will be kept on the fireplace mantle. You won't have to go anywhere. I'll be with you all the time!" It turned out to be the best decision he could have made.

I worried about what would happen to his urn once I passed on. How do you decide that among four children? Then I asked him, "When I die, I want to be buried: in a casket, in the ground. Do you mind if our children put your urn in my casket, so we can be together?" He thought that was a great idea. We stated this in our living wills.

Pastor Dave agreed to perform the service, and we discussed the location. Helder felt it should be at the church we attend because so many good family memories were there; however, it only held about 300 people. We decided we would probably have it at the sister church, which held closer to 550.

The End of Life Option bill was signed into law by Governor Jerry Brown in October of 2015; yet, it did not go into effect until June 9, 2016. Helder asked to set up an appointment with our family therapist Kathy Egan, and he wanted the whole family there. Once we were all together, Helder told the kids the bill had passed, and when the time came, he wanted to exercise his right to die with dignity. He told them there was no cure for his cancer, and no hope for prolonging his life without drastically reducing the quality of his life. He went on to explain the way the bill was written, he must be able to take the medication himself, which meant he must be able to swallow and be well enough to keep it down. Helder said this was only an option, but one he would like to take, so we could avoid the pain of watching him suffer. The suffering he said, could go on for weeks, and they undoubtedly would end up wishing he would die, so he could be out of his misery. He wanted to avoid what happened to his brother. He wanted to spare our children from that. Then he asked if anyone had questions, or if they had an objection to this decision. They all said they understood, and it was his choice to make.

One of our children asked how he would know it was time. Helder replied, "When there is no longer quality left in my life, when suffering is the only thing I'm able to do, then I hope I will know." He went on to explain that he would continue to fight for life if there were options. He also hoped he would die peacefully in his sleep. He reiterated the medication was only an option, but one he was very glad he would have, if all went well in acquiring the prescription. By the end of the session, we all had tears in our eyes.

On April 10, 2016, when Helder complained of another headache, he said there must be something wrong because he had excruciating pain in one spot. His primary physician said he should go to the emergency room, there was a chance the cancer metastasized to his brain and he could be experiencing a brain tumor. At the time, it seemed like such an extreme thought, and highly unlikely. Just the same we went to the ER and an MRI was ordered immediately.

Here we were, once again, in a hospital room. Helder was dressed in a hospital gown, with me sitting in the chair by his bed, holding his hand. It was early Sunday morning. The kids were all at their respective homes, sleeping. After the test, we sat patiently waiting for the results, and Helder said he felt a little better after taking the two extra-strength Tylenol before we left home. Finally, the doctor came in and said Helder had several brain tumors, one larger one and two smaller ones. There was nothing they could do for Helder in the emergency room and he didn't know if we wanted to do anything at all, since Helder had metastasized bilateral tumors in his lungs. He suggested if we didn't want to pursue any options, he could just send him back home with heavy pain medicine. We just stared at him. That didn't seem like a good idea.

The doctor suggested that Helder be transferred to the neurology department at USC Norris Comprehensive Cancer Center for a more thorough evaluation. Holding Helder's hand, I said that sounded like a better option. The doctor made arrangements for the transfer. Once we were alone, I asked him if that's what he wanted to do, realizing I spoke up without hearing from him. Helder replied, "Yes, let's see what USC has to say about the brain tumors. I want to take everything into consideration. I don't want to just go home with heavy meds and wait to die."

For the first time in a long time, it felt good there might be some help available. We were both feeling it. Even if it meant dealing with brain tumors, it felt encouraging to know doctors were interested again in his cancer. We had been joking for so many years, every sharp pain, "might be a tumor" that it was almost anticlimactic to hear it was one. After enduring the painful experience of planning his funeral, then discussing *how* he would like to die, dealing with a few brain tumors suddenly felt optimistic.

Helder's head was really hurting again when a nurse popped her head in the room and asked, with a sweet smile,

"Would you like a little morphine?" as if she was asking a little boy if he wanted a cookie. Helder said, "That would be nice for the pain; but I had a bad experience with high doses of opioids after surgery. Is there something else I can take?" The nurse replied the morphine was readily available, and anything else might take a while to order on a Sunday. She went on to tell him if he closed his eyes right after he was injected, and didn't move for about ten minutes, he should do all right. She would only be giving him a small dose.

The doctor returned and told us Helder would be taken by ambulance to the ICU unit, where a team of oncologists and surgeons would take further tests to see what could be done. They prepared him to be transported. We were back in the game again.

Chapter Eleven

Gamma Knife Radiosurgery

The ICU room at USC cancer center had, among other things, large floor-to-ceiling windows overlooking the city, half a dozen computer screens with scrolling data, and a $5,000 mattress creating constant movement to prevent bedsores. Before arriving at the hospital, I stopped by the house to let the children know what had happened and where Dad was. One by one we made our way to the sprawling hospital in downtown Los Angeles.

A team of doctors, surgeons, and an oncologist quickly advanced upon Helder. He had his brain scanned several times in that one afternoon. When I arrived, I saw my husband propped up in the ICU suite with six doctors around his bed. Once again, he was holding court, but this time he was asking questions about his brain tumors. I could see it was exhilarating for him to have a team of doctors reviewing and analyzing his health, especially after the discouraging response he received when he was looking for a surgical solution to remove lung tumors. That had left him feeling hopeless. Now, he was hopeful. Initially the doctors agreed on traditional whole brain radiation. (The consensus among his cancer support group was that whole brain radiation was a double-edged sword. It might have a good response rate preventing new tumors from growing, however, it often left various types of brain impairments.) Then the doctors decided to surgically remove the tumors. This ended up not being the best option because of their location. The largest one was near the optic nerve, and surgery would put Helder at risk for blindness. As it was, his vision had been worsening (i.e. the apparition of a nonexistent ceiling fan in his peripheral vision), and the largest tumor explained these vision problems. Another test revealed he had lost his peripheral vision. In the end, the team decided on Gamma Knife radiosurgery. This type of radiation, performed with a laser, not a knife, radiates just the tumor, leaving the rest of the brain intact. The doctors told Helder that this treatment would not shrink the tumors; but, it would prevent them from growing. When Helder and I were finally alone we just stared at each other. "How about that? Just when I thought I've done it all, Gamma Knife radiosurgery comes along!" he said. It was an awkward feeling to see him optimistic about a procedure to suppress tumor growth, knowing the tumors would stay there, and that more were likely to appear.

That afternoon, Helder was scheduled to have a long, intensive MRI of his brain. It was necessary to get an accurate scan which meant doing so in various spots. Helder's head had to be braced inside a cage, so that he wouldn't move during the scan. This caused a lot of anxiety for him, so they had to give him a large dose of the sedative, Ativan. Even with that he still had a lot of distress. When Helder asked if they could put him to sleep they said he had to be awake to take the necessary pictures. The staff kept increasing his dose. When they finally took him back to the room, he was completely knocked out and slept for several hours.

Later that evening, Helder had quite a few visitors. Most of them were friends from his twelve step programs; others were from his cancer support group. They were all amazed how courageous he was to have Gamma Knife radiosurgery. Everyone believed it to be a new procedure, when in fact Gamma Knife radiosurgery has been around for decades. Someone took a picture of Helder that night in his hospital bed with his close friends around him. Then, everyone went around the room and shared a memory of Helder. Liz from the co-dependency support group shared, with tears in her eyes, about her first meeting the year before. He had welcomed her with such genuine kindness and enthusiasm. She felt compelled to come back and was certain it was his warm welcome that made her feel comfortable being there. Helder had been the inspiration for a small group of members to go out to coffee and dessert after meetings. Sometimes God sends a messenger to intervene just long enough to inspire others on their journey. That was Helder in so many people's lives. At this point, he was truly there to be of service.

The next morning the procedure was performed without incidence. Helder came home later that same day with Frankenstein-like scabs on both sides of his head, because he had to be screwed to the head bracket. Eventually he lost a big patch of hair on the back of his head. He didn't know it until one day someone said he looked cute with his bald spots. He immediately felt embarrassed because he didn't know they were there. When we gave him a mirror, he was surprised. "Why didn't you tell me I had two bald spots in the back of my head?" We told him that next to Gamma Knife radiosurgery, it didn't seem to be something to bring up. Life seemed to snap back to normal. Jennifer enrolled in an advance nursing program; Rebecca was studying at California State University, Los Angeles, and Rachel was finishing her junior year of high school. Helder continued taking drops of morphine for his breathing; though it continued to get worse and an oxygen concentrator was delivered to the home. It allowed him to take oxygen in through nasal tubes. It was a large machine, and even though it sounded like a ventilator when it was on, it helped when Helder couldn't quite catch his breath and had already taken pain meds that day. Helder severely limited himself in his opioid consumption.

Tristan offered to request a delay for starting boot camp, but Helder did not want him to put his life on hold; he hoped he would still be around by the time Tristan completed the thirteen weeks of training. The morning Tristan was to report to the recruiting office, the three of us sat and reminisced about the fun times we had together. No one said it, but it felt like we wanted to have closure just in case Helder's health took another turn for the worse. We all had tears in our eyes before leaving the house, and Helder told Tristan one more time how proud he was he joined the Marine Corps. That alone was a great accomplishment in his eyes. Helder and I drove Tristan to the recruiting location, walked him to the office, and briefly met the recruiting sergeant. We took one last picture of Tristan with his recruiting sergeant, exchanged hugs with our son and walked out of the office. Helder saw a nearby store he said he wanted to look in. It was diagonal from the USMC office. While we were in there, he kept looking in the direction of the recruitment office, hoping to catch one last glimpse of Tristan. Finally, Helder said, "Let's just go." As we walked away, Helder started crying uncontrollably. He was afraid he might never see Tristan again.

Helder asked me to see if the USC Oncology Department had a referral to a specialist for managing the growth of the tumors in his lungs. He was hoping the Gamma Knife radiosurgery could also work on them. A new oncologist told us gamma knife radiation could not be used on the lungs; however, there was a new pill form of chemotherapy called Stivarga. It was only dispensed to patients with stage IV metastatic colon cancer. (This was the drug that Dr. L. had told us about months before.) Helder had told the doctor, "My son just went to boot camp, and I'd like some extra insurance I'll be here when he gets out in thirteen weeks." The doctor replied, "There are no guarantees; however, it might prolong your life." Helder started the new chemo treatment in May of 2016. The side effects were not as bad as traditional chemotherapy with the exception of fatigue. Stivarga made Helder very tired. Unfortunately, the outcome rating for this type of chemotherapy was poor. Most people had to stop treatment because it lowered their white blood count. My husband was willing to try anything.

As time went on, Helder's pain became more unbearable. Whether it was the new chemo drug or something else, we didn't know. The new oncologist followed up with scans to see the effect of the new chemo. The good news was that the lung tumors had stabilized and had not grown since the last scan. The bad news was that the cancer had metastasized to the bones in his pelvis and hip. That explained the mounting pain

Helder was having in those areas. The doctor informed us that radiation to the bone could inhibit the growth of those tumors, and Helder might get some pain relief. He asked if Helder had a prescription for morphine at home. "I'm well stocked," he told him. Unfortunately, since he developed metastatic bone cancer while on chemotherapy, there was a high probability that chemo would not be effective with the bone cancer metastasis.

After the appointment Helder told me he felt he was running out of options. He asked me again to pursue the aid-in-dying medication. He said, "With brain tumors and morphine, I no longer have the mental or physical stamina to figure out how to get it. You do, so I need you to do that for me. Will you? I don't want to drag this out any longer than I have to." I told him I would. How could I turn down this plea?

Soon, a radiation oncologist, who had reviewed Helder's scans, confirmed that he would be able to administer radiation treatment to the areas which had bone cancer. Helder was marked with a black pen and told to return three times a week for treatments. The treatment itself was not painful; but lying flat on his back was excruciating.

By now, he was in constant pain, whether he was sitting or lying down; he had difficulty breathing and used the oxygen concentrator at night; he endured weekly radiation treatments, as well as subsequent MRI scans. All the while, a veil of anxiety surrounded him. Yet, when Rebecca graduated with an Associate in Arts degree on May 14, 2016, Helder travelled to San Diego for that special day. It was also the day that convinced him to finally get a disability placard. When we arrived at the UCSD where the ceremony was held, the available parking was miles away, and drop off in front was not allowed, unless, you had a disability placard. Although I had been telling him to get one, he was afraid it would send a discouraging message to himself; he felt the placard should be reserved for those who were worse off than he was. From where we were forced to park, we had to climb hundreds of steps to get to the seating area. Helder had to stop several times; he was panting and afraid he might panic. At the next doctor's visit, I got the form signed, and Helder finally received the parking privilege he deserved.

On Memorial Day that year, we had our usual annual BBQ and invited a few of our closest friends. Traditionally, we have a water balloon toss, and I was surprised to see Helder standing on the lawn waiting for me to be his partner. We looked at each other and knew. His look was a declaration to the world, "I'm still here, and I'm going to make the best of my life for as long as I can."

Chapter Twelve

Aid-in-Dying Medication

While interviewing various hospice agencies for palliative care, Helder discovered there was a common philosophy towards end-of-life pain and suffering. Every hospice agency he met with agreed the patient's comfort was most important. When a patient was suffering to the point where pain remedies alone could no longer ease the pain, the nurses all confirmed that the patient is given what is known as "palliative sedation." This sedentary state allows the patient to sleep comfortably, until the organs shut down, and the body dies. This was the unspoken fact of hospice care, which Helder was familiar with from his brother's experience. Helder did not want to die in that manner. For him, it was a covert way to end his life. He had spent the last twenty-eight years in recovery learning to be honest and straightforward. Even more, it felt out of his control. That would be an unfair ending when there was an alternative option, one in which he could decide when and how his life would end.

On June 9th, the aid-in-dying drugs would become available. The Coalition for Compassionate Care's website was helpful with information in preparing for that day. The website suggested to start the paperwork well in advance because of the amount of time it takes to complete it. We had no idea. The first step is to request the drugs from your attending physician, the physician the patient spent the most time with. That is the doctor who will confirm all the eligibility requirements are met, which includes: being a California resident, eighteen years or older; and mentally competent, (capable of making and communicating healthcare decisions) and diagnosed with a terminal illness which will lead to death in six months or less. The request must be made twice, no less than fifteen days a part. The second step is to get verification from a consulting physician, one who is outside of the primary care physician's medical group, confirming the attending physician's information. The third step is possibly being evaluated by either physician for mental competency, but only if there are doubts of the patient's competency. The fourth step is obtain the prescription from the attending physician. The final step is for another adult, or witness, to ask the patient before he ingests the medication, if he knows he has the right to change his mind, and then having the person sign this last form. Each step must be well-documented, including signatures on all of the forms.

The attending physician would be Dr. Sheldon, Helder's primary care physician who oversaw his health as it declined the last five years. The nature of an HMO is that you must see your primary care physician first, before receiving a referral to any subsequent specialist or surgeon, making her the closest physician to his medical condition. Helder made that first telephone call to Dr. Sheldon, which was both nerve-wracking and frightening. She said she supported the law; however, she would need to research if she would be able to execute his request, since she is under contract by her medical group, as well as a contract with the insurance carrier. Both would need to agree to allow her to sign the forms and prescribe the medication. Helder became very worried. It was already sounding very bureaucratic. Telephone calls went back and forth. Dr. Sheldon told him the insurance company had no opinion either way; but her colleagues in the the medical group advised against her participating in signing any of the forms. They were afraid of the legal ramifications and did not have policies in place to protect themselves. We asked when that would happen, and they were not sure; in the meantime they forbade their physicians to sign any of the End of Life Option forms. During this phone conversation, there were tears from both sides. Dr. Sheldon knew how much Helder had suffered, and how hard he had fought to enjoy the time he had left. She supported the new law; but her hands were tied. Helder was scared he would lose the opportunity to take the drug. He felt boxed in a corner. Then he was outraged. He was counting on her to start the ball rolling. We looked at our other options.

We went to Dr. L. at City of Hope, and he said he would not feel comfortable signing the attending physician form, because he only saw Helder once every other year and for only less than an hour. In the weeks that followed, Helder and I listened frantically to the news, and I researched the internet for updates. A well-known insurance company stated they would support the law; unfortunately, we could not transfer our insurance to them, and they didn't take outside patients.

A Dr. S., whose office is near San Francisco, made a

public statement that not only did he support the new law, he would help patients complete the necessary forms, even going so far as to list himself as attending physician. Helder did not feel right with that option. He really wanted Dr. Sheldon to initiate the forms since she had been his doctor and was significant in the most crucial part of his illness.

Eventually, Helder called her back and told her he was relying on her. He needed her help, and since she supported the law, he felt that she should step up and put up a fight with the medical group. It was his "right to die with dignity" speech. After more angst and tears, she said she would help him; however, another concern came up for her. She realized she was also afraid of the backlash this might have on her medical practice and her family. After all, she explained, there were groups who opposed this new law, and they could potentially be as threatening as the anti-abortion groups who had been in the news. This was something we had not considered. We were reminded of the pro-choice doctors who had become targets for the anti-abortion hate groups. Helder did not wish to put Dr. Sheldon in harm's way, after all she was doing for him. Dr. Sheldon said she needed some time to take all of this into consideration. She assured him she was in his corner. In the meantime, she had received a telephone call from a news reporter, from a public radio station. She was writing a story about the new End of Life Option Act with questions for Dr. Sheldon on how she was planning on handling patient requests. Although the doctor did not wish to comment on it in public, she thought the news reporter might be able to help Helder in his quest with making headway on completing the necessary forms.

The next day I spoke with the reporter and explained our predicament. She was very kind and supportive, and said she would love to do an interview with Helder for public radio. He would be able to state his case, and the problems he was having getting the paperwork completed. Later that evening when I told Helder, he said, "I don't think it's a good idea to go public with my decision. I don't want someone who's opposed to the new law for religious reasons hearing the interview, and then taunting or saying hurtful things to the children in the hopes of changing my mind." Once again, Helder remembered the guilt and shame he had endured as a child because of his parent's distorted religious beliefs. He also said if he did a radio interview, he would probably have to mention Dr. Sheldon's name. It would be hard not to since she brought him to the reporter, and she was at the very center of his difficulties getting the forms completed. Helder knew he was breaking new ground with this decision, and he knew the repercussions that go along with making unconventional choices. Then he told me, "You can talk about it after I'm gone, but I don't want anything or anyone interfering with our lives, or my decision. Once I'm gone, then go ahead. The facts surrounding the process should be told – need to be told."

I told the reporter Helder would not be doing the interview. It hit me that as much as Helder loved having an audience, and this could indeed be his fifteen minutes of fame, his children and integrity mattered more to him. Then I contacted Dr. Sheldon and told her the reporter wanted to interview Helder, but he declined, as it would be hard to tell his story without mentioning her or the medical group. She thanked us for the foresight, and said she would immediately draft a letter to the medical group director, appealing their decision. In the meantime, she asked me to see if the palliative care doctor seeing Helder at home would be able to complete the paperwork.

The palliative care agency sent their doctor to our home. She was wonderful in convincing Helder to take more morphine to help with his breathing, and the pain from the bone cancer. Yet, when it came to the aid-in-dying prescription, Dr. C. told us her agency had no policies or procedures in place to support this new law. They were scrambling to get something in writing for their attorneys to review; without it, her hands were tied. Helder became visibly frustrated. He had been waiting and watching since Governor Brown signed the bill on October 15, 2015. Helder could not understand how the healthcare industry could be so ill-prepared in responding to a new bill which took effect on January 1, 2016 and was given another six months to implement. He realized at that point the road to administer the approved drug was riddled with roadblocks and red tape. Helder felt if it were a drug to prolong one's life, the medical community would be falling all over itself to get it implemented and administered. Why was there no sense of urgency in honoring the people who needed this drug to end their lives? That's when he began to wonder how much the moral issue played into the delay of carrying out the bill. As if she read his mind, the palliative doctor responded, "The agency supports the new bill. We believe it is necessary and humane to have the aid-in-dying medication available to patients who have less than six months to live. Still, without a policy in place, I cannot write you a prescription. In addition, none of the nursing staff can be in the room while you take it. We can come in afterwards and check your vital signs, but that's the extent of our involvement. For legal reasons, it has to be this way for now." Then she reminded us, the bill states no one can be forced to participate in any part of the process if they are unwilling. Helder shot me a look as if to say, there's the loophole.

Shortly after that conversation, we received a call from Dr. Sheldon. She had completed her letter to her medical group, and wanted his approval. She also asked him to write a letter of his own. She drafted her letter to the medical group, stating her case.

Dear Mr. T.,

I am an internist working at a family medicine facility in Pasadena, CA. I'm coming to you with an appeal to let me help a patient access the new end-of-life act. I have appealed to the current medical directors, and while they are somewhat sympathetic, their policy at the moment is that no doctor can participate in the new law for any of our patients.

Let me tell you a little about my patient, Helder Pereira. He is a 54-year-old who was diagnosed with metastatic colon cancer eleven years ago, and I have been his primary care physician for more than five years now. (Our office takes care of his whole family.)

At the risk of sounding hyperbolic, Helder has been one of the most inspirational individuals I have had the privilege to know, let alone to doctor. Throughout his long illness, he has been fiercely determined to live his life to its fullest. That would sometimes mean stopping or refusing chemotherapy when it made him too ill. For someone dying, I have rarely seen someone more fully alive. The prime goal of his life has never been just to prolong, but to preserve quality over quantity.

On April 20th, he scheduled an appointment with me, informed me that this bill would come into law June 9th and asked whether I would help him with aid-in-dying. We had a long, emotional discussion where he stated that he was still enjoying life, that he wasn't depressed, that he valued every moment, but that it was important to him to have control at the end. This was not about fear of pain; he understood that hospice could control pain, but he specifically did not want that at the expense of his mental clarity and loss of control. He had watched his brother die (under hospice care) and it had been a prolonged, heart-wrenching process. He wanted to be able to spare his wife and children from watching him die like that. He had spoken at length with his wife, four children and extended family, and all supported his right to choose this.

I was initially ignorant of the law and the process, but told him I would look into this, educate myself and try my best to help him. In partner with a consulting doctor, I am now ready to act as his attending doctor under the new California law. When I found out that our medical group had made a decision not to allow their doctors to participate, I asked whether I could see Helder for cash or whether there was some compromise possible that would allow me to help this dying man while still respecting the medical group's rules and regulations. Unfortunately, we were unable to come up with a solution. The family considered switching him out of HMO, but that would mean that the entire family would lose their health care coverage.

last resort I am appealing to you – someone
ᵥ a visionary and who has encouraged even the
ₑst member of his organization to come forward. I
understand that my medical group may still need time to
analyze this new law and set up ethics meetings/protocols.
But this man literally does not have time for that. Mostly,
I sense fear and caution on our part. I understand that. I
am terrified myself; I just don't think fear is a good enough
reason to hold a dying man back from what will relieve his
suffering and anxiety.

The medical group is unwilling or unable to
provide for this man what he needs and what he should be
able to obtain rightly under the law; at least allow me to
provide this for him without fear of repercussion to myself
or to our family medical facility.

I will close by asking you what you would want
for yourself or your family member should you have the
terrible misfortune to be in such a situation. As Governor
Brown said, "I do not know what I would do if I were dying
in prolonged and excruciating pain. I am certain, however,
that it would be a comfort to be able to consider the options
afforded by this bill."

I look forward to hearing back from you as soon as
possible given that this is a time-sensitive issue.

Sincerely,

Elana Sheldon, MD

Helder was touched by Dr. Sheldon's plea for compassion on his behalf. Even if he didn't get the approval, at least one professional understood what he was trying to accomplish. Shortly after the letter was submitted to the healthcare group, Dr. Sheldon was given the green light to see Helder on a cash basis, as an individual outside of the healthcare plan. The second step, which proved to be less difficult, was finding a doctor to sign off on the form as the consulting physician.

We approached all the same doctors as before, letting them know Dr. Sheldon would sign off as the attending physician, so they would just be endorsing or confirming her findings. Unfortunately, none of them felt comfortable signing the form. One doctor, the one dispensing the Stivarga to slow down the growth of the lung tumors, responded, "Why would he want to do that? The chemotherapy is slowing down the growth of the tumors!" This remark was made even after it was explained that the aid-in-dying medication was to be used *at the end* of the patient's life to shorten his suffering. We tried to explain that according to the law, the patient must request the prescription while he was still deemed mentally capable. Eventually he must ingest it himself while he was still physically capable. With multiple brain tumors now in play, Helder had a very real concern the cancer would debilitate him before he could get possession of the medicine.

Finally, Dr. Sheldon remembered a doctor who was a progressive thinker, her friend Dr. P. He heard her situation and agreed to sign the form. I instantly recognized the name from seeing him the previous year for a second opinion. The only problem was he was getting ready to leave on a three-month trip out of the country to volunteer his services. The irony wasn't lost on us. The one doctor we found who was compassionate enough to see Helder was getting ready to board an airplane out of the country to pursue his passion. His office said he would be available after hours, the day before his flight was to depart.

Helder was very nervous because this portion of the form was an evaluation of him as a patient, and if he didn't pass, then he wouldn't get the necessary signature. Dr. P. started off with a line of questioning which at first seemed combative. He asked Helder if he felt he was giving up hope; if he was aware the medical community was looking for new cancer treatments. He asked him if he thought his family would rather have him alive longer, even if it meant him suffering, and if he was pursuing this option to avoid the natural progression of dying. There were some very painful, yet insightful questions, and after a while, we were wondering if he was in fact agreeable to the law, or if he posed as being an advocate and was really there to talk Helder out of following through with the Death with Dignity Option.

Finally, Dr. P. explained, he was playing the devil's advocate. Personally, he supported the new law and had no problem signing the form. Regardless, he felt it was his duty as the consulting physician to make sure Helder had thought all of these important questions through. Dr. P. said he felt it was his responsibility to make sure Helder knew the immense responsibility he was being given. Finally, after several hours, Dr. P. signed the forms. He gave Helder his personal cell phone number and urged him to call if he had any questions at all.

The next step was to meet with Dr. Sheldon for a final evaluation. She told us she wanted to give him a basic test for mental competency. Since he had brain tumors, some still active, she wanted to make sure it was documented he was mentally competent to receive the sedatives she was prescribing. In the waiting room, Helder took my hand and said he was nervous about passing this test. He knew he had become forgetful, sometimes lost his train of thought, and couldn't remember things as quickly as before. I looked at him and said, "My strong ox of a man, these are all side effects of knowing you are dying. You are overwhelmed with emotion, anxiety and worry. This does not make you mentally incompetent. It makes you human."

We were called in and Helder passed the tests. Some of them were simple memory tests, asking questions such as, "What's your name?" and "How many children do you have?" Helder told me later he wanted so badly to throw in a joke but knew it was not the right time. He told me, "When she asked my name, I wanted to reply, 'My name is Tony Montana,'" the lead character in *Scarface*. Helder had perfected the Sicilian accent and impersonation from back in his "previous life". That's how he was; in the most frightening, scary situations, he couldn't help but see humor in it. Dr. Sheldon wrote out the prescription. We went down to the pharmacy located in the lobby of the building. She had called down ahead of time to make sure they stocked up on the quantity. We paid $750 in cash. We went home and placed it in the safe in our basement. That was on June 22, 2016. As it does, life went on, and as it turned out, God wasn't finished with Helder yet.

Chapter Thirteen
They Return

When Helder first received the aid-in-dying medication, he thought he needed to immediately determine the date for taking the medication. There were many hoops people had jumped through, legally and emotionally, to assist him in receiving the prescription. He felt it was only right that he move forward in executing his part in the process. However, as weeks went by, and life went back to a normal cadence, we stopped talking about it, and it was gently put in the back of our minds.

Helder continued to take the Stivarga to slow down the lung tumor growth. Radiation resumed to slow down the bone tumor growth. He took morphine for pain and Ativan to help with his breathing. Helder told Tristan in a letter that he had started a new chemo drug, so he could be around to see him graduate boot camp. Tristan wrote back, "Don't worry Dad, I have my prayer group praying for you." Helder's eyes welled up with tears, and he told me, "I don't think I've ever felt prouder of Tristan. He has a prayer group in boot camp! My work as a dad is done."

On July 22, 2016, after thirteen weeks in boot camp, the family drove to San Diego to watch Recruit Pereira graduate and become a Marine. I had shirts made with Pereira Family on the back. After various ceremonies, the moment came when all the families were gathered around the five battalions, containing close to three hundred Marines, waiting for them to be released to see their families. Thirteen very strenuous weeks had gone by. Within that time, there had been no guarantees Helder and Tristan would ever see each other again, and nothing seemed to keep the cancer from growing and invading Helder's body. When the moment came, and the drill sergeant yelled the command to be released, Tristan desperately started looking for his dad, and Helder made a beeline right into the group of Marines. When they finally found each other, they hugged, and both began to cry. They held each other for a very long time. No one there could have guessed how deep those tears went. They were tears of joy and relief. As if to say, "We made it."

Tristan's five best friends also came to San Diego to watch him graduate. We all went out to dinner to celebrate. Helder had stopped the Stivarga about two weeks prior. He would have been too weak to travel if he had continued with it.

After boot camp, Tristan flew to Virginia to study at the National Geospatial-Intelligence Agency (NGA) to pursue a career in geospatial intelligence. Sometime in mid-September, Helder felt he might not make it to Christmas, which is when Tristan would fly home again. It hurt my heart to see him despaired by this, so I scheduled a trip to Virginia to visit Tristan. Helder's health continued to deteriorate, but he felt he could still travel. Besides, being the family travel agent after all these years, I knew Virginia in the fall would be beautiful. Then I squeezed in a quick road trip from Virginia to New York. Helder looked genuinely happy I was going to make this last-minute request happen. He became overwhelmed with emotion, which he often did during this period of his illness.

While we were driving, Helder asked to stop by Costco so he could get Tristan some things he might need to last him the seven months he would be stationed in Virginia. He started putting a coffee maker, a music speaker, and a TV in the cart. Tristan tried to stop him and told him he didn't have to buy him all of this. Helder looked at his son and started crying. He said, "It feels good to be able to do this for you. Please don't take that away from me. I don't know if I'll be able do it later." The three of us hugged in the aisle. We left and continued our road trip. The weather was perfect, and the short trip, which included a Broadway play and dinner in Little Italy, went smoothly. Helder's longtime friend, Gina, met us for breakfast, and afterwards took us to Times Square where the play was showing. We accidently walked in the wrong direction and had to go around one more block. Helder didn't think he could make it. His breathing was labored and going around a New York block in Times Square had all the makings of a panic attack. I told him we didn't have to rush, and together we slowed down the pace. He made it, but after the play we took a bicycle carriage back to the hotel.

Helder's headaches became more severe, so when we returned home he had a follow-up MRI to check on the progress of the brain tumors. He had felt strange sensations in his head, the squiggly lines he saw overhead never went away completely, and his peripheral vision got progressively worse.

On October 18, 2016, Helder celebrated 28 years of sobriety. He asked his daughters to present his cake at the regular Friday night meeting. We had dinner first with a few close friends. I noticed Helder was not his usual self. He was a lot quieter and more reserved. He no longer held court, recounting funny stories and twelve step anecdotes. His pain was constant, and he preferred not to take take much morphine when he was out of the house. *Especially when accepting a cake for being sober.* Intellectually, Helder knew it didn't interfere with his sobriety. Prescriptions were not only a necessity of life, they were encouraged by fellow members, so he could take it guilt-free. He had more than enough lectures from doctors about the effects of pain on the body and the mind. He knew it was better to address the pain than to allow it to get out of hand. Emotionally, it had been a point of pride to be drug free, and Helder wanted to be in control of that area of his life, since he had no power over so many others. He decided when to take the pain meds and going out with friends was not one of those times.

There was a sense of anticipation and dread leading up to the day of the exam. MRIs had become so anxiety-provoking Helder could barely sleep the night before. He dreaded having his entire body inserted into the machine, with just his feet sticking out. It was as if Helder had held it together for so long, and for so many years, that he just couldn't do it anymore. What we didn't know until we got to the MRI floor, was that since Helder was having the diagnostic test as an out-patient at USC, there were no sedatives available to give him. Helder looked visibly alarmed, so I spoke up when we were checking in and I told them, "My husband is claustrophobic and cannot proceed with the MRI unless he has a sedative." They asked if he had a prescription for Ativan or Xanax. I said, "Yes, but it's at home."

This meant we had to wait for a doctor to write a prescription, then walk two buildings down to the hospital pharmacy to fill it, and then back again to the location of the MRI. This delay increased Helder's anxiety even more. I held his hand as we waited. All the while Helder was in pain from sitting. The bone cancer caused excruciating pain any time he had to sit upright for any length of time. Waiting rooms are notorious for having upright chairs with very little padding. We got through that day and returned to the oncologist's office for the results. We were shocked to discover he had three new tumors, one of which had previously been treated with the Gamma Knife radiosurgery yet was growing. The doctor explained they could use the Gamma Knife on the new tumors; but the largest tumor, which had already been treated, could not be treated a second time. He asked if we wanted to see a neurosurgeon for a second opinion.

The new doctor did not look like a typical neurosurgeon. He was young and had a hipster way about him. He also had a practical attitude and approach. Helder liked him a lot. Immediately, we felt we were in the right hands. He was very bright and at the same time, warm and even a bit charming. He reviewed the MRI scan for quite some time before telling us, "I think I can surgically remove the largest tumor. It is not a cure, you will still have the other brain tumors; still, it's your only option and it may prolong your life." There was that pause, then Helder said, "This is fantastic news!" The surgeon looked at Helder and smiled, tilting his head looking a little perplexed. Helder asked, "Is there any reason I shouldn't have this surgery?" The doctor replied, "There are the usual risks, but no. It's just most of the patients I see are not that enthusiastic about having brain surgery." Helder's optimism hadn't run out. Not yet. Of the three new tumors, the two new ones would undergo Gamma Knife radiosurgery, and the largest one would be removed.

When we met with Dr. Sheldon again, we did not see the same enthusiasm from her. She reminded us that Helder had numerous tumors in both his lungs, along with a difficult time breathing. She did not believe he was a good candidate for surgery, especially one that would involve general anesthesia. You could almost hear us deflate. We went back and forth about it, and it was our turn to be perplexed. It was ironic that two years prior, Helder practically begged thoracic surgeons to remove tumors from his lungs. Now, he found a surgeon who seemed unconcerned about removing a brain tumor. Overshadowing all of this was our beloved doctor who was looking at his overall health, and was responsible for weighing the outcome of such a surgery. It was this primary care physician who reminded Helder his primary concern was quality of life. She explained he might do well while under general anesthesia; however, once the oxygen tube was removed from his lung, there was a possibility his lungs would be too weak to start breathing on their own. They could become dependent on the ventilator for oxygen. Dr. Sheldon agreed to see if Helder could pass a physical which would indicate if his lungs would bounce back and breathe on their own when he came out of surgery. Helder was gravely concerned about becoming ventilator-dependent. He most definitely did not want that outcome.

Helder and I talked about it day and night for several days. Finally, he decided not to take the chance, and would rather let the cancer run its course than be left on a ventilator.

The very next day when we told Rachel, she looked surprised and said she thought he would give the surgery a try. She quickly said she supported whatever Dad wanted to do. That evening, Rebecca came in to talk with her dad, and he told her what he had decided. She started crying and said, "You're not even going to try? Removing the tumor could give you more time here with us."

Later that night Helder told me he felt he had to go through with the surgery. He asked if there was a document he could sign which would give the directive to remove him from a ventilator should he become dependent. I told him we could write it on his health directive. He said, "Carol, I need you to promise me you won't leave me hanging on a ventilator. I don't want my life to end that way."

Miraculously, Helder passed the lung test, and the surgery was scheduled. First, he had to undergo Gamma Knife radiosurgery for two of the tumors the week before surgery. Tristan flew in from Virginia. On October 20, 2016, the six of us went to the hospital very early in the morning. We were all so nervous. The possibility of losing him either in surgery, or because of the anesthesia weighed heavily on all our minds. While he was being prepped for surgery, he still found a way to make us laugh with his jokes. When it was time for him to go, each child gave their Dad a hug and we were all visibly shaken. When he was wheeled away to surgery, we were told it might be four or five hours before we heard anything. Several hours later, the surgeon came into the waiting room and told us the surgery went as expected. We asked if he recovered from the anesthesia, the doctor said he left him while they were still "closing him up." The anticipation was unbearable.

As soon as we received Helder's room number, we went to see him in the ICU. We slowly walked into the large room and in the first bed we saw a man who looked a lot like Helder, on a ventilator. My mind froze. *Is that Helder?* Then we heard a voice from around the corner, "Can you get me some more ice chips, please?" It was Helder sitting up in a bed located in the corner. We broke out in smiles and hugs; we were so happy that he had not only survived the anesthesia, but had also undergone a successful surgery.

The next afternoon, they put a knit skull cap on Helder's partially shaved head and sent him home. The high from the success of the surgery lasted almost a week. When the reality came back that he still had cancer, the depression started to creep back in again. The surgery gave Helder the illusion he was going to get well. That is what is *supposed* to happen when you undergo surgery. This was just giving him a little more time. He still had excruciating pain in his hip and pelvis; he still had difficulty breathing, and he still had compromised vision.

Now that Helder knew it was possible the brain tumors could continue to grow, even after Gamma Knife radiosurgery, he felt surrendering to the brain cancer was unavoidable. It felt good. Helder was thoroughly exhausted both mentally and physically. He never wanted his loved ones to feel he was "giving up", but this time he knew he was done. He had given his battle with cancer his all, until there was nothing left to give. Once he did surrender, he felt calm and could finally live with a heart of peace. Fighting a battle he had already lost only created more anxiety and unrest for him. At this point, he was really in hospice mode, even though he would never call it that. He just wanted to be comfortable and enjoy the company of his family, which is why I was caught off guard when Helder said we should still have our annual pre-Thanksgiving Open House. I knew he had no energy to get the house "party ready," so I was a little concerned how it was all going to come together. Helder sought the help of his children. Tristan had flown back to Virginia where he continued study at the NGA, but when he returned home for Thanksgiving break, he helped as much as he could.

On November 19th we threw one more pre-Thanksgiving Open House, where we provided turkeys, roasted chickens and ham, and asked our guests to bring their favorite side dishes to share. We had an amazing turnout from his cancer support group, soccer friends, twelve-step program friends, childhood friends and neighbors.

The party started at five p.m. and didn't end until nine or ten o'clock. That evening, for the first time ever, Helder left his guests early, and crawled into bed around eight o'clock. He had no strength left in him and his breathing was agonizing.

Chapter Fourteen
December 26, 2016

Movie openings for the holidays were always an exciting time for Helder. Every year we discussed which movie would be our official "Thanksgiving Day Movie", and our "Christmas Day Movie." In 2016, there were so many movies he wanted to see. He would tell me, "I hope I'm still around to see *Passenger*." Or, "I really want to see *Collateral Beauty*. I hope to see that one." Sometimes he would pause and say, "I'm really going to miss this world. I can't believe I'm going to miss *Guardians of the Galaxy 2*." He had accepted years ago he wouldn't be able to see his grandchildren or walk his daughters down the aisle. The things he missed in December were the immediate day-to-day adventures of life. He literally started living one day at a time. Contemplating anything past that was too difficult, both mentally and physically.

The month of December was filled with movie outings for the Pereira family. There were a few caveats: always at reserved seating theatres and always with reclining seats. Helder couldn't sit for two hours upright in a regular theatre seat. It all had to be just right.

Early that month, we went to a restaurant in Old Town

Pasadena. It was one we had been meaning to check out and realized *now* was the time to do it. It was the two of us and our three girls. Helder had lost his voice and was whispering at that point. We were sitting in a booth, finishing up our meal when suddenly, he whispered, "I'll meet you back at the car." Rachel went with him. Later, I found out he was having a hard time breathing. He felt he was too far from home and panic started to set in. I told him to remember to take his anxiety and pain medicine for breathing. He reminded me that he hates to take it when going out in public. I reassured him, "I can never tell by the looks of you if you've taken it." There were no outward signs he had taken anything. But *he* knew, and he didn't like it. I realized that may never change. He would have to stay home more and more, so that he could get the pain and breathing relief he needed.

At some point I contacted a school friend whose nephew's stepmother used the aid-in-dying pills just one month after the medication was available. Her nephew had told her I could call him with any questions. I knew it would be helpful to get as much information as possible, so that Helder's last days were a smooth transition.

The nephew was very kind and informative. He told me it took quite a while to open all the capsules. He, his father, and his stepmother shared in the task of putting the mixture together. He also told me it was best not to be alone in case I needed help with anything. Lastly, he said his stepmother had passed quickly, first slipping into a seemingly deep sleep. All of that was so good to know. Most importantly, it felt good to talk to someone who had gone through this experience. Another one of God's miracles was being put in contact with this young man. I was extremely touched that he was willing to share and retell such a personal story with me.

Additional research of my own suggested sherbet or ice cream was handy in case the medication was too bitter, or if something was needed to keep it down. I also learned the prescription could be mixed with apple juice. There was a total of one hundred bright orange pills which had to be opened and emptied into a six-ounce glass of water and apple juice.

At bedtime, on his last night, Helder set his alarm for 6:30 a.m. He had told the kids he would take the medication at 7:30 a.m. on an empty stomach. The next morning, Helder turned off the alarm, as he did every morning for the last twenty-three years, and he took a shower. After he started the water, he came out of the bathroom and asked, "What should I wear?" I said, "I have no idea. I can't even think right now. My mind is blank. This is the hardest thing I've ever had to do." We just stared at each other for a moment. Later I realized how ridiculous that must have sounded to him. He went back into the bathroom and it came to me. I went into his drawer, hoping it was still there, and pulled out the grey shirt we wore at Tristan's boot camp graduation, the one with PEREIRA FAMILY written on it in large bold letters.

Helder continued with his daily routine, brushed his teeth and shaved. There was something so surreal about the ritual. Helder was a man of habit, and on his last day of life, he made sure he was clean. I knew it felt right because it was the way his parents raised him, and the Seventh Day Adventist way, to keep your body clean. His mother would say, "Wash off the day's dust."

When he was through, he sat in his chair in the bedroom, waiting for the kids who came in one by one. The plan was for me to slip into the bathroom, mix the medication, and then bring it out to him while he was sitting in his chair. That's not what happened. When Helder was ready, he told me to go ahead and start. I didn't realize how time consuming it would be to open 100 capsules, making sure all the powder got out of each capsule. It was taking much longer than I thought. The capsules were packed tightly, so they had to be rolled back and forth with my thumb and index finger. I kept worrying what would happen if I didn't get all the powder out. My biggest fear was that if the medication didn't end his life, it would instead leave him in a coma. Helder and I had talked about that possibility, and how horrific it would be for the children to see him slip into a coma, not knowing if he had died or not. I needed help and I knew instantly there was only one other person to help me. After about twenty minutes, I opened the door and asked Helder to come in and help. He came into the bathroom and together we opened all 100 capsules. When we were done, he meticulously cleaned the counter with a cloth saying, "I don't want anyone accidently getting any of this into their system." I was throwing away the empty capsule shells when he said, "I'm just going to drink it now." Our eyes met. My mouth opened, but nothing came out. He was drinking it. He stopped when he was halfway done to say, "I'm going to need that sherbet." I yelled out, "Get me the sherbet!" Someone ran off. Seconds later, the sherbet was brought in. I put it on the counter, closing the door behind me. "Helder, please go sit down in your chair. I'm getting nervous." I couldn't get over the fact he veered away from the plan and drank it right after we mixed it. "You were supposed to drink it in your chair," I said, feeling numb and faint. Helder said, "I'm afraid to take it out there. Someone might accidently drink it." I was dumbfounded. How could he be worrying about a far-fetched idea at a time like this? "Please go now and sit down. You're going to feel it soon," I begged. He finally left with the sherbet in one hand. He had tried to think everything through; all the angles, so we wouldn't get hurt. He was a hero in every sense of the word. I joined him back in the bedroom, and put on the Leonard Cohen song, "Hallelujah" and we gathered around him.

After he was gone, I called the hospice nurse, and she came to check his vitals and pronounce him dead. Everyone was crying. We slowly walked out of the room, one by one, and sat at the dining room table. Rebecca grabbed my arm, and looking right into my face said, "Now what are we going to do?" I gently told her, "We're going to try and get through this day. Then we'll get through the next. Just one day at a time." Kenny Lamm handed out excerpts about grieving, and we started talking about the process. We would surely have been lost if it weren't for Kenny. He guided us through that first hour. I couldn't let my mind go there in all the years of planning, what it was going to be like that day, that first hour. While we were waiting for the mortuary personnel, I suggested that the kids might want to spend a little time with their dad before they take him away. I told them it was believed his spirit was still there; that it leaves slowly. Each one of us spent time alone with him. When it was my turn, I knelt next to him and cried, "I can't believe you're gone, Helder. My only prayer is that you know how much I love you. And know I will take care of our children." They were the most important part of his life, and I instantly felt honored to be his wife, the mother of his children. When I left his side, I knew in my heart he had left this world in peace.

That afternoon I had to make the most difficult phone calls of a lifetime to Helder's friends – our extended family. Social media played an important role in getting the word out that he had passed away; I was able to reach out to people I would never have been able to find. This included Edmilson who said he would be coming to the memorial service with his wife and son. When they arrived the morning of the service, he told us that meeting Helder had changed his life. By hiring him and his brother to help us with the new house, it afforded him the opportunity to go back to school and become a minister. From there, he joined the Navy as a Chaplain. It was a touching testament to Helder's life.

On January 7, 2017, memorial services were held at the Pasadena campus of Montrose Church. It was a cold, rainy day. The family was escorted into a small room just off the main sanctuary. For a building that held 550 people, there was "standing room only." When it was time, one of the ushers walked us out into the church. Tristan wore his Marine dress blues. The initial shock of seeing over 600 people gathered for the services was overwhelming. Helder had impacted so many people's lives: childhood friends, his soccer family, who wore soccer jerseys in his honor, sober friends and neighborhood friends who brought their entire families. Kenny and Scott gave a tribute, and each of our children read their Christmas letters. The reception hall was next door, and there was a line of people as long as the church waiting to pay their respects to the family. Later that day, the pastor shared with us that he had never seen this many people stay after a service to meet the family. It took extra time because each person got a hug from me in remembrance of Helder. That is how he greeted everyone. I soon discovered that people waited in the line to share with me the positive effect my husband had on their life. I heard so many stories and anecdotes that day. During the reception, we allowed family and friends to share a memory of Helder. Several soccer kids came up, some of his cancer support friends did, too. A lot of his sober friends shared funny stories. All the while, a slideshow played on television screens throughout the reception hall. The first one was comprised of Helder's friends, starting with him as a teen, and ending with friends he had known for over thirty years, now in their fifties. The background music was Bob Marley singing, "The Redemption Song." It was one of Helder's favorite songs, because it echoed his life.

The second slide show showed photos of family life, starting with current family pictures and ending with Helder's mother and father in Brazil at a Seventh Day Adventist church service. The background song was "Somewhere Over the Rainbow" sung by Israel Kamakawiwoʻole. When we went to Hawaii in 2008, just five months before Helder's mother passed away, we were sitting in the plane waiting on the runway when this song came on the overhead speakers. Both Helder's mother and father, who had been divorced for over thirty years by then, insisted on coming with us to spend vacation time with their grandchildren. Helder had reached over to hold my hand and he nodded to where they were sitting. We then looked at our children. In that moment everything was perfect. Our hearts were full, and we were beaming with gratitude for our family. Since then, that song had a special meaning for us. Dreams really do come true.

I always knew planning your own funeral arrangements was one of the most selfless things a person could do for the loved ones they left behind. It didn't really hit me until I actually had to go through the motions of coordinating my husband's funeral. Helder was such an intricate part of our family, the sudden loss of not having him to talk to left me numb. Having the arrangements planned, from the mortuary to the church service, was enormously helpful. It allowed us to carve out the necessary time to be alone and grieve our loss, instead of having to make all those arrangements.

All those years while I was focused on relieving Helder's pain, especially when it was so excruciating at the end, he had been focused on relieving our pain. Now I know, exercising the End of Life Option was the bravest, most selfless act Helder did, and the ultimate show of love for his wife and children. Following are the letters Helder's children wrote to him that Christmas:

Dear Dad,

YOU ARE MY HERO. "Mom is that going to be my daddy?" The best line I have ever said. God spoke through me that day. I can't put in words how much you mean to me, and how much you impacted my life. You are a blessing; God put you in my life as my Dad. You are a definition of a father figure and so much more. I love the person you are and how you live your life. You are a great example of how life should be lived. You showed me a way of life through the principles you live by.

I love you so much; you are the strongest person I know. You are an amazing person. I have so many great memories with you, and I will always cherish those. I remember every day after school you would pick me up and make sure I would get 100 percent on my tests – which I did. I would write spelling words repeatedly, so I could get a perfect score on my spelling tests (that practice helps me today on how to memorize things for tests). Thanks to you I know my multiplication table and how to read. I would read to you out loud even when I didn't want to, and you would still push me to do it. Thank you for not giving up on me, Dad. Thank you for teaching me how to ride a bike. That video is my favorite! That is a perfect example of what an incredible dad you are. Thank you for teaching me how to drive in the Costco parking lot. Thank you for making me stretch every day for ice skating. Thank you for taking me to ice skating practices and dance rehearsals. Thank you for coaching me in soccer and softball. Thank you for being a cool dad. All my friends loved you. You know how to make everyone laugh. It is so fun being with you. There is never a dull moment with you. Thank you for helping me fix things when I call for help. You are the number one handyman; you know how to fix everything that is broken. Thanks to you, I like classic rock music. I know who sings what songs as you use to quiz me when songs came on the radio. Thank you for being so patient with me. Thank you for visiting me in treatment and going shopping with me. That day meant a lot to me. Thank you for not giving up on me. Thank you for being understanding. I want to be like you and live by your morals and values. Thank you for getting a boat, so we could go camping and do water sports. Thank you for opening your house to summer and birthday pool parties. Thanks to you, I know who I can go to and trust that they can be there for me. Thank you for letting the house be open to my friends and including everyone. I don't know any person who doesn't like you. You are so likeable and funny. You are good to be around. You are one of a kind and unique. I look up to you in so many ways, Dad. You don't have to say anything – it is your actions that show how great and amazing you are. You are a walking miracle. You are strong and courageous. When you are feeling weak and tired, you still pushed through. I admire you so much for that. You are the reason why I do not give up on life and still work for what I want to accomplish.

I will always love you, forever.

Jennifer Hope Pereira

Dear Daddy,

You have always been there for me. Through the ups and downs, the silly fights and the hard times, you are AL-WAYS there. No matter how upset or how angry I am, you know how to calm me down. You get me.

If there is one person I know I can count on in my life, it's you. You have been, and always will be, the most important man of my life. You have taught me so much about life. You've helped me look at things from a different perspective. You've helped me turn even the most negative situation into a positive one. That has made me a better person.

One of my favorite memories is when you put me in as goalkeeper during our playoff game. I was so afraid I would cause our team to lose. But you taught me it doesn't matter, as long as I know I did my best. Of course, it helped that we won the game. But I will always remember how you had faith in me. That was a better feeling than winning.

You are the strongest person I know, and the definition of *No Fear*, which was passed on to me. Since I was a little girl, you've put me on skis, dirt bikes, boats, soccer fields, and even horses. You taught me to show up for life.

Just like the song, Daddy, "You light up my life, you give me hope, to carry on."

I love you,

Rachel

Dad,

Nothing I say to you will give justice to the insurmountable respect and love I have towards you. You have always been and always will be my hero. I idolize you. As a man, I try to emulate you in every possible way, because you are what it means to be a man. You have touched so many lives that it feels like you have been blessed with such love and wisdom. I want to be like that. I want to be the father you were to me. I want to sign my son up to Boy Scouts and go backpacking and camping with him through the rain and snow. I want to take my son dirt bike riding through hills and long trails over mountains. I want to teach him how to ski and watch him snowboard like he's on fire. I want to teach my son how to play soccer, coach him and mentor him, and be with him on adventures around the country playing soccer with amazing teammates. I want to take my son and his friends out on the lake, watching him wakeboard, then try to throw him and his friends off the inflatable. I want to take my son and his friends camping with my family, so I can grow to love his friends. I want to fill my son with so much love that he knows what real love, kindness, and patience is. I want my son to spread his love in my image, always remembering the face of his father, because this is what you have done for me. I only pray that I am and always will be my father's son.

I love you, forever and always.

Tristan Josler Pereira

Dear Dad,

I look back on all the school field trips where you made everyone around you laugh. I remember you as my father, knowing that I was always safe with you as my protector. Having you as my soccer coach and making you proud as I scored a goal or defended one. I remember all the times you would let me read to you while you were cooking in the kitchen. You helped me with words that I couldn't pronounce. I remember you teaching me about lessons of self-acceptance, bravery, love and life. So, I want to thank you for making me invincible, and for showing me I could be and do anything my heart desires in this life. You loved me no matter the weather, rain or shine. And that is all that I could ever want from you as my dad. Thank you for showering me with gifts when all I truly needed you there by my side, journeying through life one step at a time. I think the worst part about all of this is the fact that there is no one in this world who will take care of me like my dad will. Who will install a zipline in our backyard just to see us have fun? Who would try his best to make sure that I never get hurt, and raise me to be the kind, strong, and lovable comedian I am today? But, I am also grateful for moments like these that allow me to truly feel emotion, love, and pain, because that is real, and it is the most important part of my life with you. Today, I love sharing my stories, life experiences, struggles, and achievements with you, because I always know that you are sincerely interested in how my day went, or what I found beautiful about a certain movie. I could always count on a deep connection with you, because you saw the true meaning of what life is really about. It's about planting trees, making connections...oh, and most importantly, quacking life away. I love you with all my heart and will continue to love and cherish you as being the most remarkable dad this life will ever know. Love indefinitely.

Your miracle,

Rebecca Viana Pereira

As for me, I didn't prepare anything personal for the service. I felt there were no words and not enough time to convey how I felt about my life with Helder. That was when I realized I had to write this book and tell his story. The process of putting together this book has been cathartic for me and my family in our healing process, and has helped us work through our grief.

We hope that our experiences navigating the healthcare system can inspire others on their journeys to take the reins of their own care.

Epilogue
One Year Later

There is definitely an invisible line separating my life before Helder passed, and after. So many things I didn't anticipate. I didn't know I would hurt so much. I thought knowing he was going to die would soften the blow, but it didn't. It felt almost shocking once he was gone. I couldn't get over how I thought I would do better with the grief. It was pointed out to me that I couldn't possibly have known because I'd never experienced losing him before. You can only imagine how you're going to feel, but don't really know until it happens. Life without Helder has been really hard. There has been a constant pain in my heart. A real, physical pain.

The biggest revelation which I didn't plan on is how much I had learned from Helder. He was the one who fixed things that broke. Once he was gone, I found myself doing things I had no idea I could do. I went around the house with a hammer and screwdriver fixing things; figuring out how to get the grass in the yard to live again, negotiating on home repairs; all things he taught me without realizing it. I showed up to places even though I'd rather stay home because he taught me to appreciate life. There are so many things I've pushed myself to do with him in mind. To say his spirit lives on is a very true statement. I'm living it. At first the realizations made me sad; I wished I could tell him how much he had taught me. I started wondering, had I ever stopped to tell him how clever he was? Then it came to me one night that I had told him. I remembered we had met with his therapist before we got married, to make sure we were both moving forward with our eyes wide open. It was important to Helder for us to have that one session. I was a little perturbed about it, thinking he had reservations about getting married. The therapist asked, "Helder, why is it important to you we have this meeting?" He looked at me and said, "I want to know why you would want to marry me. It's not like I have a lot to offer." I sat still, and listened to my heart. I told him, "Because if I were stranded on an island, or there was a worldwide disaster, and there was just one other person who survived, I would want that person to be you. I would feel safe with you, knowing you could and would take care of me. You are brilliant in so many ways, and can fix just about anything. To top it all off, you would do it with a sense of humor. Humor is always just above the surface with you. More than all of that, you have a heart of gold. I've seen it with my own eyes the love and compassion you have for people. Most importantly, I actually like you. I like who you are. And that makes you the man I want to marry."

Words from Kenny Lamm

Eulogy for Helder

"Just a couple days before his leaving us, Helder and a couple of his kids and I were whispering to each other in his room. We were discussing God's power as it related to healing and recovery. Helder got all lite up and passion filled his eyes. He said there is a word that describes what I am trying to say and I can't think of it. Well, Helder's pitbull intentions took over as we all tried to guess the word, finally he whispered at the top of his lungs, STEWARDS. We are blessed to be stewards of God power. We know God's power is love and that Helder took the "careful and responsible management" of love very serious, he used it to teach us a valuable lesson. That no matter what life brings our way, we are able to handle it with grace and dignity, even death. I can only speak for myself but I know we all feel the same way, we were blessed to know Helder Pereira whether it was for a day or a lifetime and we will keep that blessing with us until we see him again.

Helder has moved on to continue to be the manifestation of charity with his higher power who has always been, is now and will be forever. If I know Helder he has already picked out the best campsite and is making sure there is plenty of room for us to join him when we arrive. I wanted to end with something I know Helder would have wanted to say to each of you, without hesitation the first thing that came to mind was... I love you. "

Acknowledgments

Dr. Elana Sheldon: You were Helder's last hope and you really came through with your letter and your willingness to help him. Thank you for being on our team.

Cancer Support Community: Thank you for helping Helder focus on "The Dash" between the year he was born and the year he died.

Kathy Egan: You were the foundation our family needed. You possess just the right mix of compassion, knowledge and spirituality. God bless you.

AYSO, Region 88: Soccer gave Helder a reason to keep fighting. Thank you all for your compassion, love, and support over the years.

A Dedication to Helder Pereira

Helder and Jennifer

The Pereira Family
Helder, Ester, Jose and Josler

Helder, Jennifer, Tristan and Rebecca

Helder and Josler

Helder and Kenny

Tristan, Rebecca and Helder

Helder and Rachel

Helder
and
Tristan

Helder and Carol

Helder's favorite vacation, Costa Rica

Helder learns a new sport